NATIVE AMERICANS
OF
EAST-CENTRAL INDIANA

NATIVE AMERICANS OF EAST-CENTRAL INDIANA

CHRIS FLOOK

THE History PRESS

Published by The History Press
Charleston, SC
www.historypress.net

Cover images: Back cover illustration courtesy of Jim Huth. Wood carving of M'sing at top middle on front courtesy of the State Museum of Pennsylvania, Historical and Museum Commission.

First published 2016

Manufactured in the United States

ISBN 978.1.46711.856.9

Library of Congress Control Number: 2016930881

The book is dedicated to the Delaware Tribe of Indians. Their perseverance, hospitality and kindness are qualities we should all seek to emulate.

Contents

Foreword

The study of Indigenous peoples in early Indiana is a history of man's ingenuity and practicality in adapting to the environment in which they lived. The early east-central Indiana groups, identified as Adena and Hopewell, are explored in this book regarding how we identify their specific culture from relics, effigies and artifacts. We can learn how they distinguished themselves from other peoples by examining these remains. It is truly amazing to see the variety and the myriad ideas in these objects, along with how they used these materials to adapt to their environment. These groups would be considered "eastern woodland peoples."

As we move from pre-contact into modern times, just after 1500 in our common era, we distinguish between tribal peoples who are identified by a specific language and culture. In our area, the Lenape, or Delaware, arrived in what would become the state of Indiana in the 1790s and had a positive impact on early state development. The Lenape, who were forced from the East Coast, also had a positive impact on Indiana with the founding of what would become the cities of Muncie and Anderson. The descendants of Lenape in Indiana—the Delaware Tribe of Indians, who live in Oklahoma—are the twenty-fifth-largest tribe in the United States and are still a viable tribe.

The study of these cultures in Indiana is a testament to their practicality and adaptability. The author presents a positive look at both pre-contact and modern tribes in an entertaining and informative way. I commend the author for his efforts to bring attention to the early history of Indiana and the cultures who helped to form it.

Wanishi ta. "Thank you very much!"

MICHAEL PACE
Former Assistant Chief
Delaware Tribe of Indians
Bartlesville, Oklahoma

Acknowledgements

Without the help of the following people, the completion of this book would simply not have been possible. I wish to thank my fantastic copy editor, Kathie Flook; Jarred Scott and Leo Caldwell for their photography; Kelli Huth for early feedback; the philologist Raymond Whritenour and language expert Jim Rementer for their evaluation; George Everett Keller and Jim Huth for their fantastic artwork; Kevin Nolan for his evaluation of Part I and his artifact dating; Cathy Carson for her artifact dating; Steve Snodgress, Matt Zacek and family, as well as Alan Flook, for access to their artifact collections; Christy Brocken, the Conner Prairie Interactive History Park, the Strawtown Koteewi Park, the State Museum of Pennsylvania and the Indiana Historical Society for providing historical images; the Delaware County Historical Society for its assistance in research; and Mike Pace for his consistent dedication and enthusiasm for Native American history in Indiana.

Introduction

There was never a Native American chief named "Munsee" living at any point in time in east-central Indiana. There were, however, chiefs named Kikthawenund, Buckhongehelas, Hockingpomsga and Tetepachsit. There was never a man named "Munsee," and the two Native American statues on Walnut Street in Muncie are unrelated.[1] Munsee refers to a dialect spoken by the Delaware, or Lenape, people. Along with their Unami-speaking brethren, the Munsee-speaking Lenape were an Algonquian indigenous culture that flourished along the Hudson and Delaware River Valleys. The Lenape were eventually pushed into Indiana after the Northwest Indian War. Furthermore, the fantastic earthworks found along Indiana waterways in Anderson, Yorktown, New Castle, Windsor and Winchester are remnants from Native Americans living in east-central Indiana thousands of years ago, whose material and burial culture archaeologists refer to as "New Castle Phase"—a localized expression of regional Adena and Hopewell cultures. I learned these facts of history and the distinction between New Castle Phase and Lenape Native Americans, embarrassingly, as an adult. Like many Hoosiers, I knew little of Indiana's post-European contact with Native Americans and even less about the pre-European cultures.

Then, as life's greatest intellectual discoveries often happen, I stumbled across Frank Haimbaugh's 1924 *History of Delaware County Indiana*.[2] While reading Haimbaugh's history, I noted the absence of a "Chief Muncie" and a distinct two-thousand-year separation between the "moundbuilders" and the post-contact Native American Lenape period, suggesting a far more

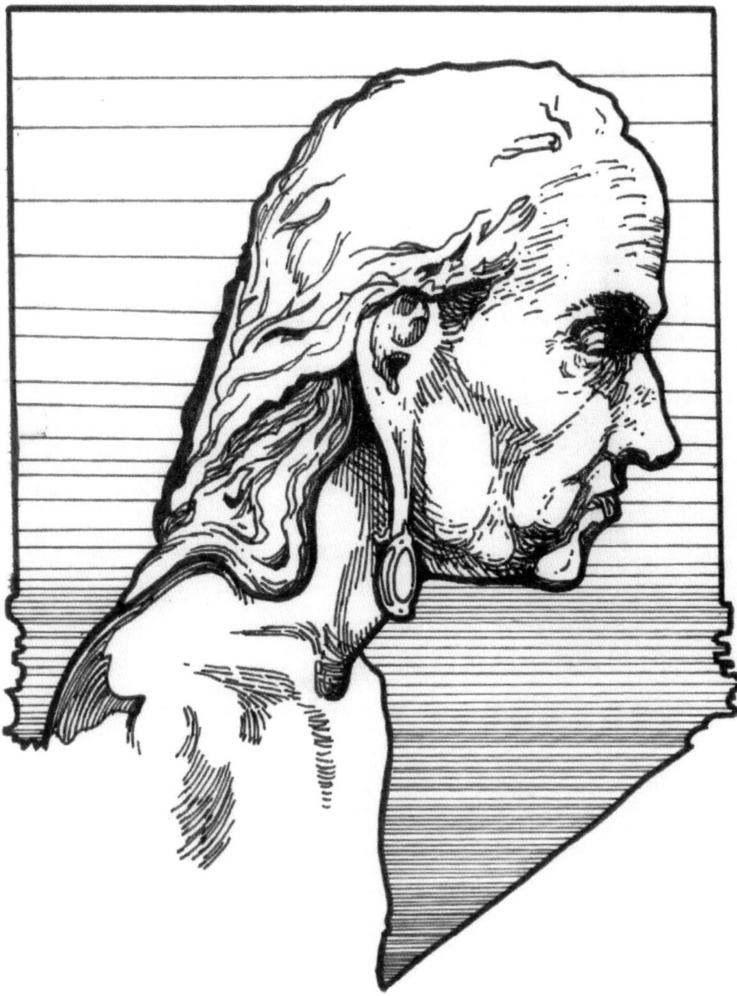

Buckhongehelas. *Courtesy of George Everett Keller.*

complex past regarding Native American history than what is commonly discussed in Indiana history books. That simple discovery has led to a decade-long investigation of Native American history and archaeology in east-central Indiana. This book is a result of that research, an overview of what scholars know about the indigenous peoples of east-central Indiana.

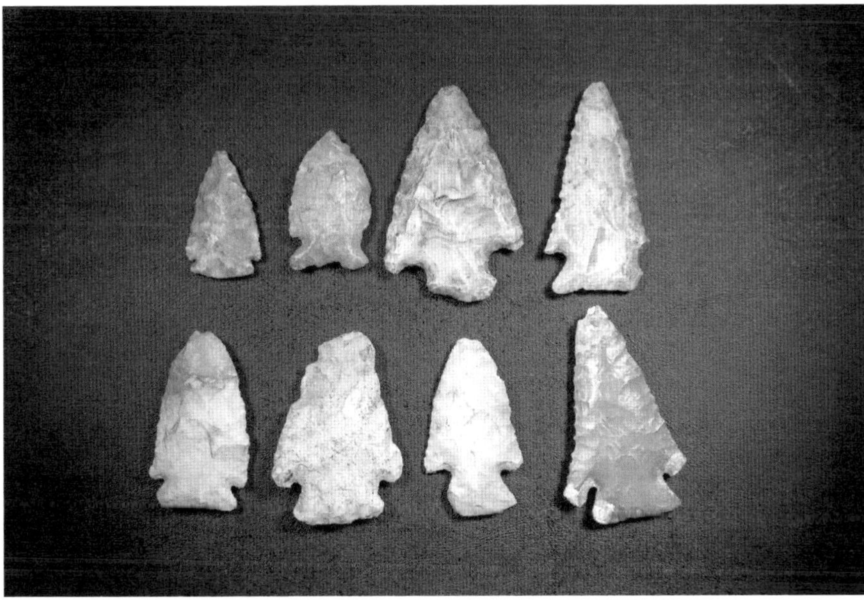

A collection of notched projectile points found in Indiana. *Courtesy of Alan Flook.*

This exploration extends back thousands of years to local expressions of what some archaeologists refer to as the Adena and Hopewell cultures and will cover post-European contact groups with an emphasis on the Lenape. This book is best considered an introduction to the culture, history and archaeological record of east-central Indiana's first peoples. Hundreds, if not thousands, of books, scholarly articles, archaeological reports, historical narratives, oral histories, settlers' tales, linguistic studies and government documents exist covering the indigenous groups that lived in east-central Indiana. For those readers interested in exploring further, an extensive bibliography is included in the back of this book, listing the sources in order to dig deeper.

The book is arranged chronologically, with Part I focusing on Native Americans in east-central Indiana living during Early and Middle Woodland Periods. Part II focuses on post European contact indigenous cultures in the same area. The latter part emphasizes the Lenape, or Delaware, peoples. While the Miami and Shawnee were active in this area, the Lenape were the predominant group living along the west fork of the White River at the end of the Northwest Indian War.

NATIVE AMERICANS IN EAST-CENTRAL INDIANA

The indigenous habitation of east-central Indiana is far longer than the period currently inhabited by modern Americans. The first non-Native people who entered east-central Indiana were probably French trappers and traders in the eighteenth century. The first *documented* non-Native people in east-central Indiana were the Moravian missionaries in what is now the city of Anderson in the early 1800s, and the missionaries indicated people of African descent at the same time. Comparatively, the first substantial evidence of indigenous activity suggests that humans were present in the area more than 10,000 years ago![3] This book will focus on Native Americans who lived in east-central Indiana during the Early and Middle Woodland Periods, beginning approximately in 400 BCE until the time when the Lenape left the White River in 1821 CE. This time frame covers 2,221 years, a substantial range of time when compared to the 216 years of Euro-American residence in the same area. More simply put, in the past 10,000 years, the place where many Hoosiers call home has only been inhabited by the non-indigenous about 2.16 percent of this time. This is critical in understanding the importance of why we must learn more about the indigenous history of Indiana. The United States is only a recent phenomenon and the history of "Indiana" is overwhelmingly Native American.

It is not uncommon for historians of European descent to place an emphasis on post-contact periods when writing the history of Indiana. The aforementioned *History of Delaware County, Indiana* by Haimbaugh is a prime example. Written in 1924, his work spans two volumes, nearly one thousand pages of material, only about fifty of which discuss indigenous history. Perhaps Haimbaugh did not care, or he simply may not have had the available historical and archaeological resources at his disposal to accurately cover the Native periods. This historical omission is more troubling when found in work from recent historians. For instance, James Madison's 2014 *Hoosiers: A New History of Indiana* has only three chapters that feature Native Americans, about seventy pages of his more than four-hundred-page book.[4] Howard Peckham's 1978 *Indiana: A History* places little emphasis on the state's indigenous past.[5] These major omissions in local history perhaps are due to a natural tendency to emphasize the history of one's own ethnic group, or maybe it is because we choose simply to ignore the vast and diverse history of the indigenous cultures in North America.

Historians, of course, can write about whatever topics stem from their own intellectual interests. However, it is downright negligent when a dearth

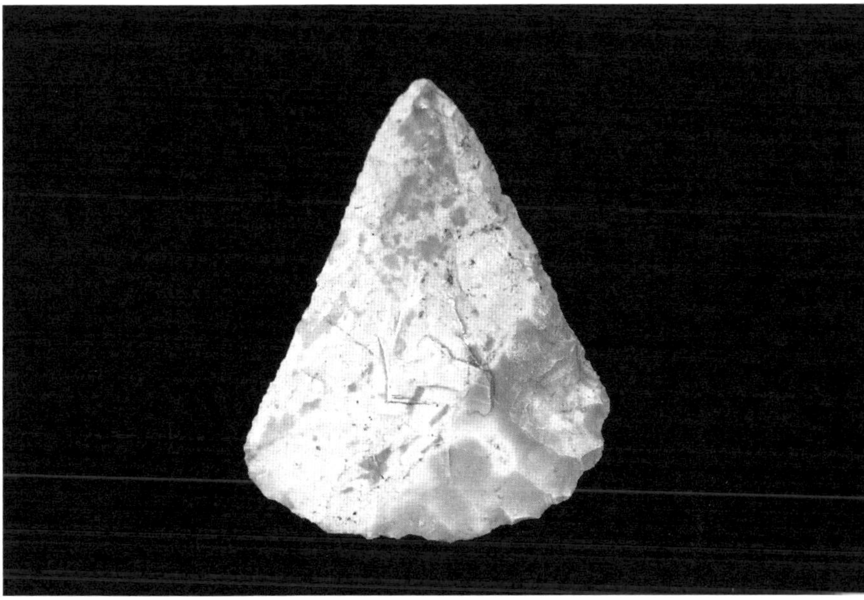

Middle Woodland Period projective point. *Courtesy of Steve Snodgress.*

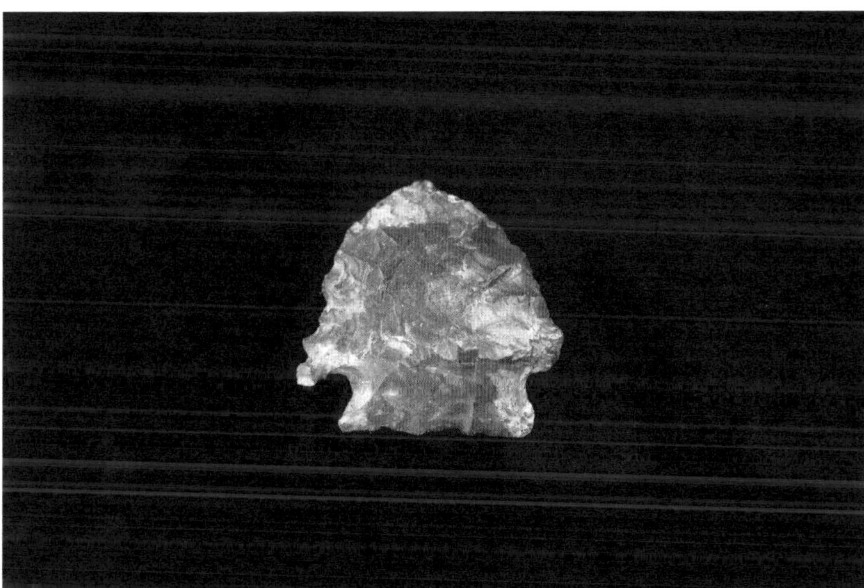

Early Archaic Period projectile point. *Courtesy of Steve Snodgress.*

of Native history exists in primary education. Indiana has eighteen history standards for fourth-grade social studies teachers that must be covered in class. In Indiana, fourth grade is when elementary school students are first taught state history. Only two of Indiana's eighteen standards are designed to cover more than ten thousand years of indigenous history.[6] The two standards require students to "Identify and compare the major early cultures that existed in the region that became Indiana prior to contact with Europeans" and "Identify and describe historic Native American Indian groups that lived in Indiana at the time of early European exploration, including ways these groups adapted to and interacted with the physical environment." Even the most gifted social studies teacher will have trouble condensing several thousand years of human history into a few lessons.

Suffice it to say, our collective ignorance of the indigenous history in Indiana stems from the lack of emphasis from historians and state educational standards, resulting in many Hoosiers not knowing Native American history in Indiana. A full, comprehensive work covering pre- and post-European contact Native American history in Indiana would require many thousands of pages. This book is therefore only best understood as an introduction to the topic in east-central Indiana.

ISSUES OF TERMINOLOGY

An avid reader of archaeological and historical literature will know that scholars often disagree on the particulars. Throughout this book, I attempt to identify areas of scholarly disagreement. These debates center on many different aspects, but deriving common nomenclature for languages, tribes, cultural groups, funerary rites and so on appears to be a sticking point most often appearing in the literature. There are many reasons for this, but the most prominent basis for disagreements originates from the fact that written records prior to European colonization simply did not exist for indigenous cultures outside of Central America. In pre-European contact North America, one way in which information is derived about a particular culture originates from the physical evidence left behind. This evidence might include human remains, tools, pottery, religious carvings, wooden structures in the form of postholes and earthworks. Archaeologists study cultures by exploring their physical remains, buried cultural materials and organic materials, such as carbonized remains of seeds, animal bones and wood fragments.

Without written records to supplement these artifacts, archaeologists are left to explain a way of life using various methods of interpretation. The farther back in time we go, researchers rely more on archaeology to explain human activity. Interpretations are constantly changing as new material is excavated in the field. As can be expected, individual archaeologists might interpret the same data in different ways, leading to varied conclusions on how a particular group of people lived. The terminology therefore becomes diverse and unique with the varying interpretations.

The arrival of Europeans coincided with written histories. These accounts, while often biased, provide modern historians with primary sources of first encounters. Early explorers and missionaries would write down their observations as they ventured across North America. For example, the Spanish conquistador Hernando De Soto[7] traveled throughout the southeastern portion of the United States in the 1540s. While De Soto himself was illiterate, a few conquistadors in his expedition had the ability to write and kept journals of their journey. In east-central Indiana in the early 1800s, a group of Christian Moravians had a mission along the White River in present-day Anderson. The missionaries kept extensive journals of their experiences as they preached to and interacted with nearby Lenape villages. While the work is full of misinterpretations, misunderstandings and religious bias, it serves as an excellent primary source, in part, to help us interpret what was happening in the lives of the White River Lenape. While these sources are great places to start reading about indigenous history, they are often inaccurate. The early colonists simply did not have the scholarly historical and archaeological training of today, and personal biases often crept into their work.

As Euro-American governments moved their people across the continent, an extensive system of administrative documents becomes available in the historical record. These documents record land transactions, treaties and prominent meetings among indigenous leaders and territorial officials. This information helps us to formulate consistent terminology, connect events and people and place specific occurrences in the relevant periods.

It is beyond the scope of this book to comprehensively explore all of the various archaeological and historical interpretations of the Native Americans in east-central Indiana. Furthermore, it is necessary for me to provide a common set of terminology when describing specific people, cultures, tribes and events even if scholars debate the precise application of those terms. Readers should be aware that the nomenclature used in this book is not universally shared among scholars in history, anthropology and archaeology.

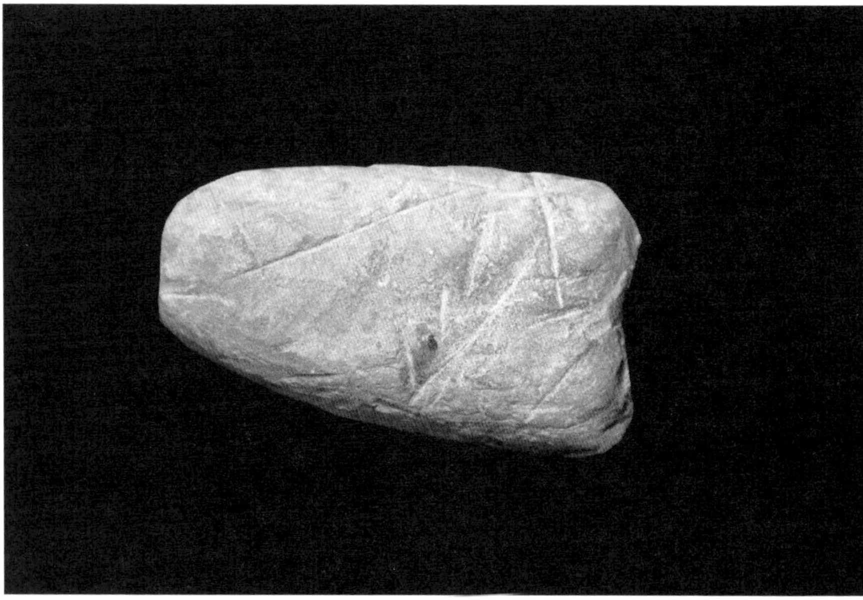

Celt fragment. Note the plow marks, indicating modern agricultural activity at the site. *Courtesy of Matt Zacek.*

I attempt to outline where scholars disagree but ultimately use a common set of terms for the sake of clarity.

It is also important for readers to know common archaeological terms used when describing ways of life, funerary practices and chronological cultural units of pre-contact Native Americans in North America. In archaeology, terms are used as units of organization in reference to and supported by the physical evidence found in the field in order to delineate periods of time and categories of associated material.[8] A resulting catalogue of artifacts reflects the people who used them in a specific time and place, and we can construct and interpret ideas on how they lived based on this evidence. As these scientists share their field findings, it becomes convenient to relate interpretations with a common vocabulary. Archaeology is not history in a narrative sense.

North American Archaeological Terminology

Unit is used arbitrarily to define a group of artifacts. In archaeology, many scientists organize artifacts within the archaeological record by time, ways of life and geographic areas. A *unit*, therefore, is a means of organization allowing us to understand different groups of people living and interacting with their environment during specific periods. A *period* is a term archaeologists use when describing a specific range of time, as defined by the archaeological record in a large geographic area, irrespective of their technological achievements. Many different groups of people might be in the same *period* of history in a geographic area. A *tradition* is a range of time where a specific group of people, or groups of people, exhibited a set of technologies, cultural traits, way of life or the creation of materials persistently over a period of time. Often in North American archaeology, *periods* and *traditions* have the same names such as the Woodland Period and the Woodland Tradition. The Woodland Period has a clear start date and end date, while the Eastern Woodland Tradition largely exists during this period but extends after this timeframe in small pockets across the eastern United States. A *phase* is used to describe an archaeological *unit* where artifacts are similar in a specific time in a local area. Finally, a *cultural complex* is a term used to describe a set of specific artifacts that show up in the archaeological record in at least two sites in a given area over a *period* of time. These artifacts then represent a specific archaeological culture. A *culture* in the archaeological sense is used to define a set of data from recovered artifacts that represent the physical remains of people living in a specific area during a specific time.

Pre-European Contact Terminology

At one point, I had considered using the term "moundbuilders" to describe the pre-European contact indigenous groups living along the west fork of the White River and its tributaries from approximately 400 BCE until 300 or 400 CE. Despite the colloquial accessibility of the moniker, "moundbuilders" is inexact, problematic and inconsistent with the terminology used by modern archaeologists.[9] The more appropriate term, "New Castle Phase," best represents the pre-contact Native Americans living in east-central Indiana during the Early and Middle Woodland Periods.[10] The problem with "moundbuilders" is multifaceted. First and foremost, the people living in east-central thousands of years ago left far more than just mounds. While the earthworks are the most noticeable evidence of habitation remaining today, artifacts of less prominence have also been found. Second, the term was used inaccurately by early histories to reference a mythical "race" of beings that supposedly built the earthworks.[11] In the 1800s, several "historians" and amateur theorists erroneously deduced that the great earthworks in the Ohio River Valley area could not have been built by the ancestors of the frontier Native Americans and, therefore, must have been built by a mysterious group of people. Early settlers simply did not understand what they came across along the waterways in central Ohio, southwest Ohio and east-central Indiana. The post-contact tribes also had no knowledge of their creation, having been separated from their construction by at least 1,500 years. As ridiculous as this may sound, it was a common interpretation for many Americans to assume that a mythical race of people had built the earthworks. Even today, there are people who believe equally preposterous notions that the earthworks were constructed by any of the following: the Lost Tribe of Israel, Welsh sailors, the Vikings and even Fallen Angels known as Nephilim.

Finally, other indigenous cultures constructed large earthwork mounds in different parts of what is now the United States and had no direct connection

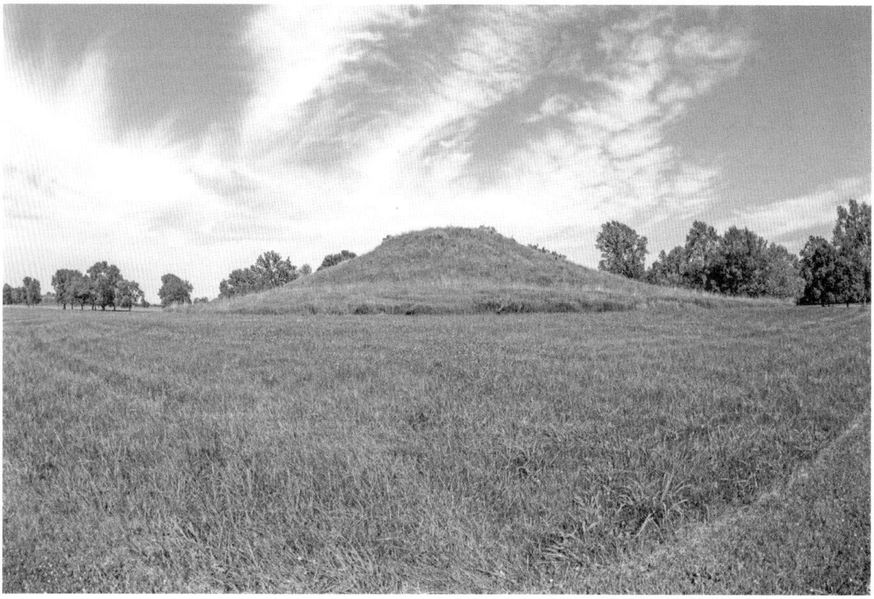

Remnants of Middle Mississippian Mound 56 at Cahokia, near St. Louis. *Photo from author.*

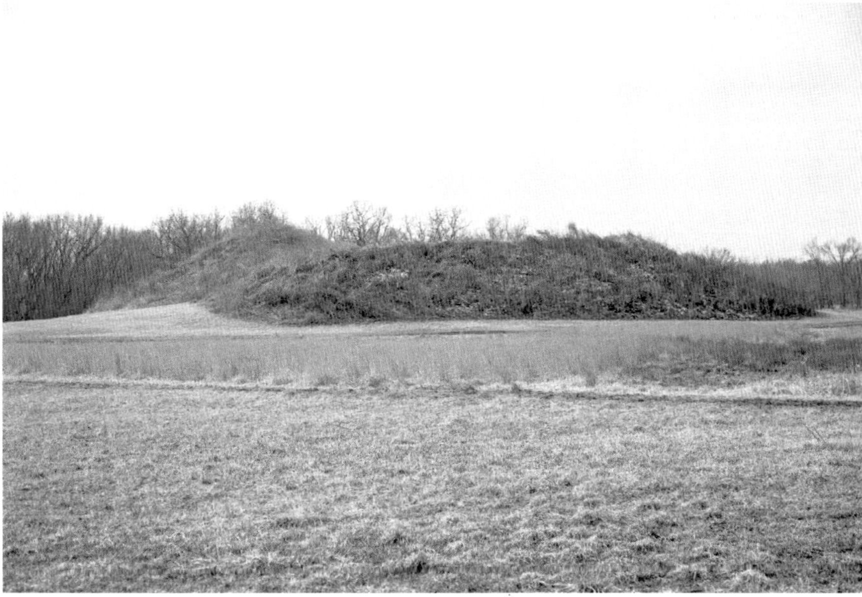

Remnants of the Middle Mississippian platform mound at Angel Mounds near Evansville. *Photo from author.*

with the groups living in east-central Indiana during the Early and Middle Woodland Periods. Centered near what is now St. Louis at Cahokia, a Native American culture began constructing large platform mounds around the year 1050.[12] These mounds were much larger than the Adena/Hopewell mounds and were often designed to house the residences of chieftains and other important structures. These "moundbuilders" are generally referred to as the Mississippian Culture. The only known earthen structures left by these groups in Indiana exist at Angel Mounds in Evansville. Chronologically and culturally, there is no direct connection.

As we shall see, many other terms, identifiers and designations, such as Adena and Hopewell, are also imprecise when applied to east-central Indiana. The names Adena and Hopewell are heavily debated by archaeologists as to their best use, with some researchers disregarding them entirely. Even common archaeological definitions of Adena and Ohio Hopewell are limited for us in that they do not precisely encompass the activities of those living in east central Indiana during the same periods. We also have no idea what the Adena and Ohio Hopewell peoples called themselves. It is also critically important to understand that Native American habitation in east-central Indiana existed before the New Castle Phase Native Americans and long after. We simply do not know enough about these cultures to adequately describe them, let alone provide distinct cultural designations. The most researched, readily available evidence in the early twenty-first century, indicating consistent habitation by humans in east-central Indiana, originates from Early to Middle Woodland Periods. Archaeologists currently define the remains from these periods as New Castle Phase. There has yet to be a comprehensive archaeological survey and analysis of pre-contact Native American artifacts before and after the New Castle Phase in east-central Indiana, despite evidence suggesting habitation. Further evidence that would shed light on pre-contact Native American culture in east-central Indiana is quite literally beneath our feet.

POST-EUROPEAN CONTACT TERMINOLOGY

For the most prominent group of post-contact Native Americans who lived in east-central Indiana, I have opted to use "Lenape" instead of the "Delaware." At the time of first European contact, the indigenous groups Europeans called Delaware lived on the Atlantic seaboard, in what we now call the Delaware and Hudson River Valleys. They had no unifying political structure, living scattered in decentralized villages. They referred to themselves as Lenape (the people). As England assumed control of the coastal areas, Thomas West, known as the 3rd Baron de la Warr, became the second governor of Virginia. The peoples living in these areas became known as De la Warr's Indians and later just Delaware Indians. Although Delaware is the name most often used to describe their descendants even today, I chose to use the indigenous autonym "Lenape," as it seems more appropriate in the context of the time. I use "White River Lenape" in reference to the specific Lenape bands in east-central Indiana from the 1790s to 1821.

This book also does not extensively cover the cultural history of the Delaware people, nor does it comprehensively discuss the Delaware tribes in existence today.[13] The concept of a "tribe" is a relatively modern term to designate the political organization of Native Americans as they coalesced in the interior of North America.[14] When Europeans first arrived in the Delaware Valley, the Lenape were a politically and geographically decentralized ethnic group, sharing a similar culture, and spoke at least three different languages. As Europeans moved inland, the Lenape were pushed into the interior and organized into a politically unified "tribe."

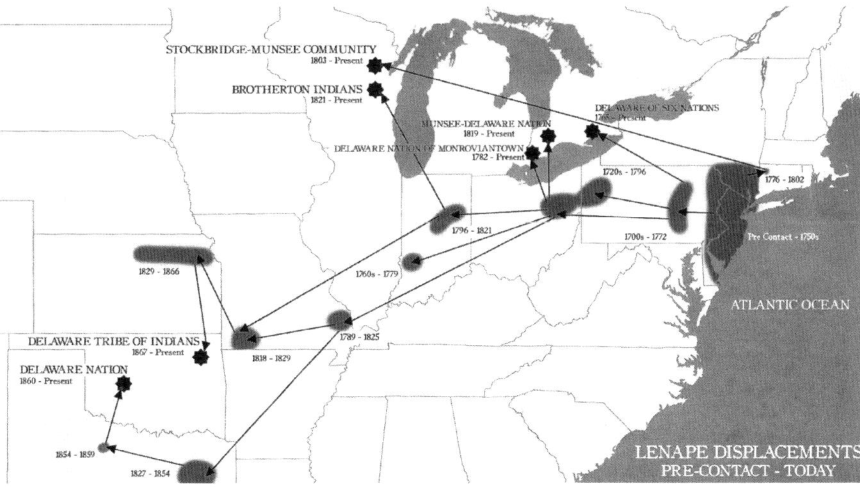

Lenape displacement, migration and current federally recognized tribes: pre-contact, 2016. *Image from author.*

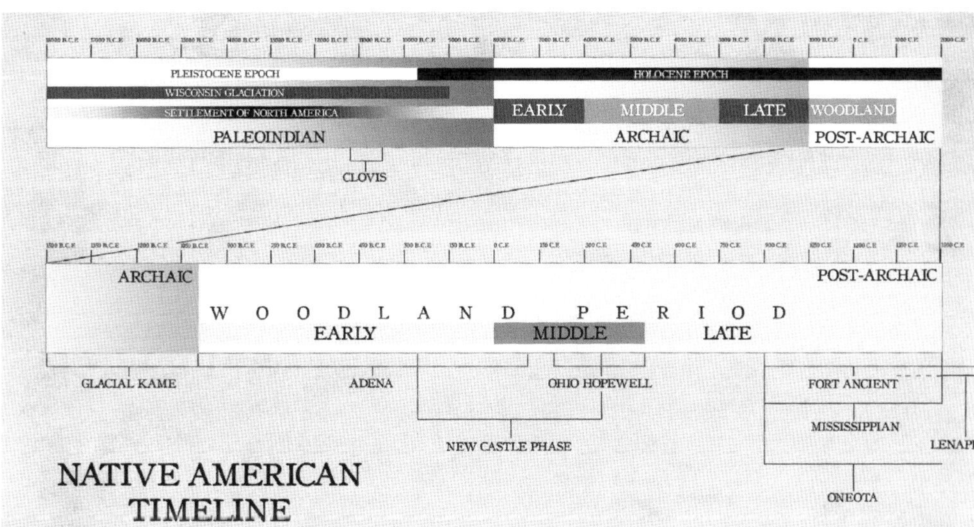

Timeline of Native American periods, Midwest indigenous cultures and east-central Indiana phases. *Author's collection.*

Over the years, various Lenape descendants formed several different political tribes, each with ancestral connections on the East Coast. Today, there are three federally recognized tribes of Lenape in the United States and three in Canada: the Delaware Tribe of Indians in Bartlesville,

Oklahoma; the Delaware Nation in Anadarko, Oklahoma; the Stockbridge-Munsee Community in Bowler, Wisconsin; the Munsee-Delaware Nation of Ontario, Canada; the Moravian of the Thames of Ontario, Canada; and the Delaware of Six Nations, also of Ontario, Canada. The State of New Jersey recognizes two tribes of Lenape: the Nanticoke Lenni-Lenape of New Jersey and the Ramapough Lunaape Nation. Several other unrecognized tribes exist across the United States. While each of these tribes celebrate their shared cultural heritage, language and ancestry, it is important to note that they are not fossilized entities of the past, but rather vibrant communities today with real twenty-first-century needs. The locations of these modern tribes demonstrate the radical dispersion in North America after European colonization. The Delaware Tribe of Indians is the tribe historically connected with the White River Lenape in east-central Indiana.

TIMELINE OF NATIVE AMERICAN HISTORY

As mentioned, scientists often organize North American indigenous groups into various archaeological units reflecting their physical remains, including periods, traditions and phases. Woodward and McDonald succinctly describe this in their *Indian Mounds of the Ohio Valley*: "Each *period* represents a span of time during which, theoretically, certain general cultural characteristics were well established and widely distributed among populations of Native Americans. The sets of general cultural characteristics shared by widely dispersed populations of native peoples are called *traditions*. Within *traditions*, we identify distinct groups by their cultural names."[15] *Periods*, therefore, are long lengths of time in which we can describe general living patterns by identifying shared cultural characteristics. *Periods* are essentially chronological units. *Traditions* are the way of life of groups of people living in a specific time and place, but the specific traditions are linked chronologically. *Traditions* may also span across multiple periods.

To understand how human beings first came to North America, it is also important to comprehend glacial activity on Earth. The human habitation of North America most likely occurred during the last period of extensive North American glacial activity. This "glacial period" saw enormous amounts of water locked as ice in moving glaciers, which reduced sea levels worldwide.[16] The lower sea levels exposed land between Asia and North America, forming the Bering Strait Land Bridge. Many people incorrectly refer to this most recent period of glacial activity in North America as an "ice age," but it is more accurately identified as "glaciation" within our current ice age, the "quaternary glaciation." Quaternary glaciation began about 2.58 million years ago and continues today. Ice ages are defined as periods of time on Earth when large sheets of ice (glaciers) grow and expand and then recede. We are currently in an ice age due to active ice sheets in the Arctic, Antarctic and on Greenland. The cycle of advancing (glacial) and retreating (interglacial) ice repeats due to Milankovitch cycles. When the ice recedes to the poles, this is known as an interglacial period. We are currently in an interglacial period known as the Holocene epoch. One day in the future, the ice will grow again, reducing sea levels worldwide, while covering large sections of North America. The last glacial movement in North America is known as the Wisconsin Glaciation. The Wisconsin Glaciation extended from eighty-five thousand years before our present time and ended about eleven thousand years ago. The Wisconsin Glaciation growth flattened northern and central Indiana.[17]

While the precise dates are still debated, it is generally accepted that human beings began crossing the Bering Strait at the end of the last glacial maximum, with successive migration waves ending around 8000 BCE. Bands of hunters and gatherers were most likely following game and foraging for food.[18] While not widely accepted, some scholars suggest that humans also colonized North America by boat from the Atlantic or even Oceana.[19] However they arrived, the early indigenous groups spread out across North and South America in the following centuries to inhabit both continents and the Caribbean islands.

PALEOINDIAN AND ARCHAIC NATIVE AMERICAN PERIODS

Archaeologists organize the first human cultures in North and South America as living in the Paleoindian Period. About fifteen thousand years ago, small groups of hunters may have begun to follow large herbivores such as mastodons and woolly mammoths across the Bering Strait Land Bridge, extending down ice-free corridors into North and South America. These groups ultimately inhabited the American continents as hunters and gatherers.

One of the first indigenous cultures identified by archaeologists living at this time was the Clovis Culture,[20] appearing in the archaeological record

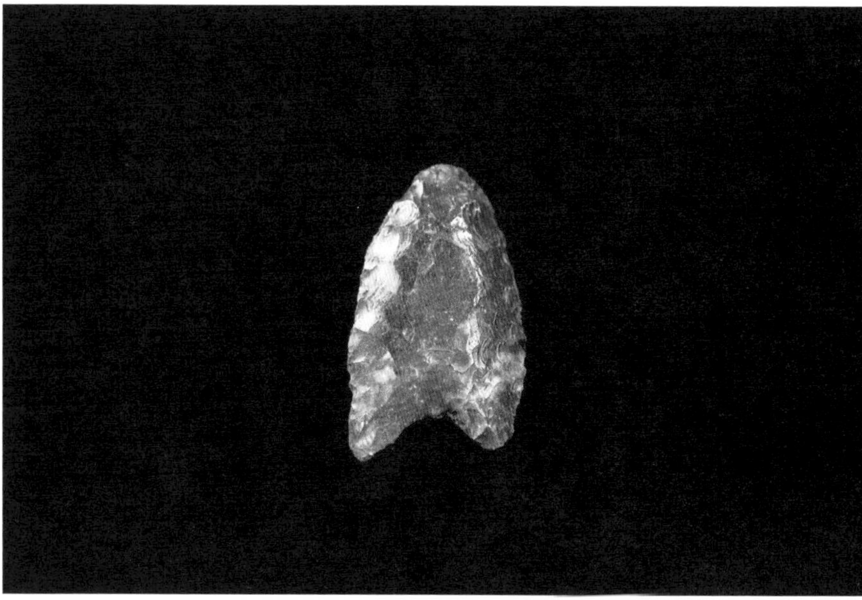

Paleoindian Period projectile point. *Courtesy of Steve Snodgress.*

about thirteen thousand years ago. Distinctive projectile points, known as Clovis points, identify this culture. Evidence of Clovis Culture exists across North America, including Indiana.[21] The archaeological record suggests that these people subsisted on hunting and gathering.[22] As the ice continued to melt, the large megafauna that helped to sustain the early indigenous Americans began to die off. Scholars debate as to what exactly led to the extinction, but the evidence is clear that the large mammoths and mastodons ceased to exist, and as a result, the living arrangements of North America's first inhabitants changed.

These changes, along with radical climatic and environmental variations, affected indigenous culture, resulting in a stark difference in the archaeological record for the period. Archaeologists organize the cultures immediately following the Paleoindian Period into the Archaic Period, lasting from approximately ten thousand to four thousand years ago. During the Archaic Period, these indigenous North Americans lived essentially as hunters and gatherers. There are many cultures and traditions identified in the archaeological record during the Archaic Period, including the Old Copper Complex and Red Ochre around the Great Lakes, the Riverton Culture in the central Wabash River Valley, the Chihuahua tradition in the American Southwest and Poverty Point Culture in the Southeast. Archaeologists also divide the Archaic Period

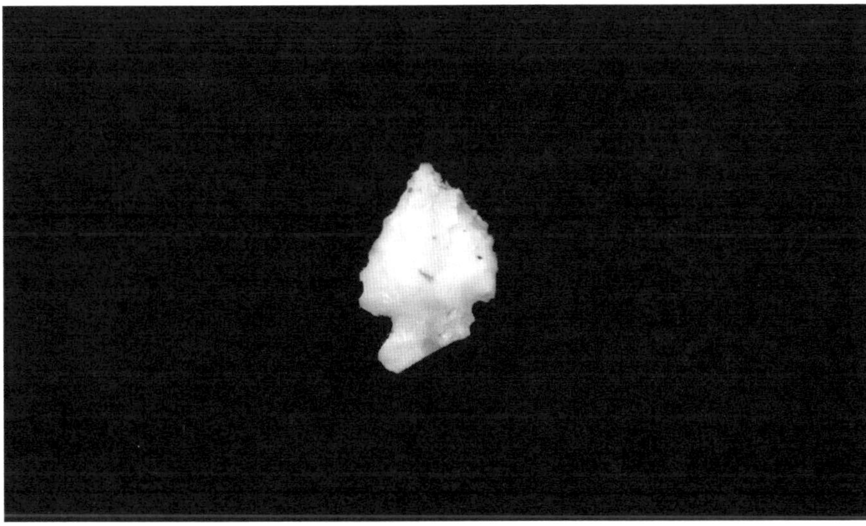

Above: Riverton point, terminal Late Archaic. *Courtesy of Josef Zacek.*

Right: Late Archaic Period projectile points. *Courtesy of Steve Snodgress.*

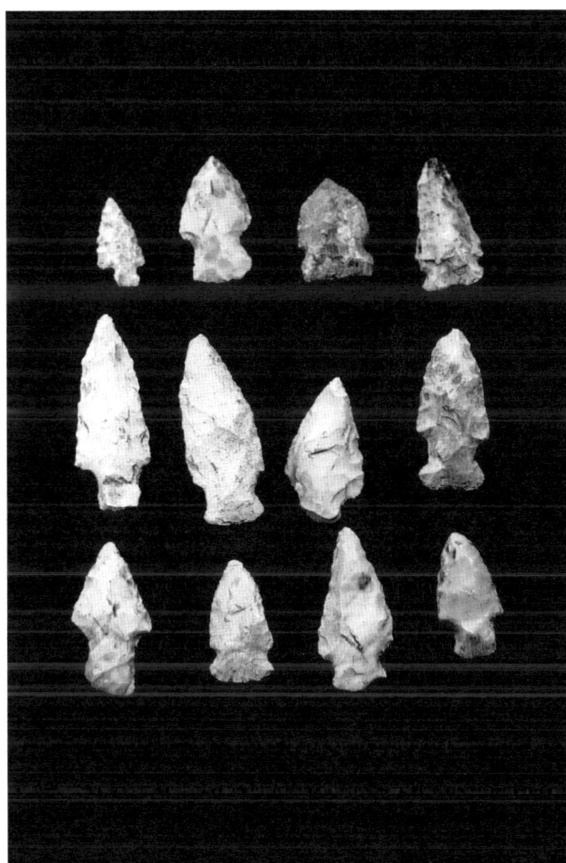

into three separate sub-periods, including the Early Archaic, 8000–6000 BCE; Middle Archaic, 6000–3000 BCE; and Late Archaic, 3000–1000 BCE. This organization of periods is designed to help *us* understand the differences in the archaeological record and is not reflective of cultural changes between, for example, the year 3001 BCE and 3000 BCE.

During the Archaic Period, the Glacial Kame Culture is known to have inhabited Indiana.[23] Those whom we identify as Glacial Kame had unique mortuary practices of burying their dead in hills and natural mounds formed by receding glaciers. These groups would cut deep graves in the sides of hills, placing their dead with burial "goods" such as gorgets and pipes. Glacial Kame peoples were primarily hunters and gatherers much like other cultures living in the Late Archaic Period. They also began small-scale domestication of plants.[24] This agricultural shift was a precursor to the more consistent domestication of plants by Adena and Ohio Hopewell peoples.

WOODLAND PERIOD NATIVE AMERICANS

Following the Archaic Period, archaeologists organize all of the North American indigenous traditions and cultures into the Post-Archaic Period, which extends from about 1000 BCE until today. The Native Americans living in the eastern half of the United States fall within the Woodland Period. The Woodland Period is further divided into the Early Woodland Period, 1000–1 BCE; Middle Woodland Period, 1–500 CE; and the Late Woodland Period, 500–1000 CE. The Woodland Period[25] is marked by a continual reliance on hunting and gathering, but with increased small-scale domestication of plants including maize, squash and various kinds of beans, although dates for the origins of domestication vary. The cultures living within the Woodland Period improved manufacturing of various tools, pottery and textiles. By the end of this period, indigenous cultures had adopted the bow and arrow. The most prominent cultural phenomenon during this period in east-central Indiana and the Ohio Valley is the construction of various earthworks, including mounds and enclosures. The archaeological record for the Early and Middle Woodland Periods in east-central Indiana contains artifacts often identified as being left by Adena, Ohio Hopewell and New Castle Phase Native Americans.

During the Late Woodland Period in central Indiana, archaeological evidence suggests habitation by distinct peoples, whose remains are identified as Oliver Phase, Western Basin Tradition, Upper Mississippian

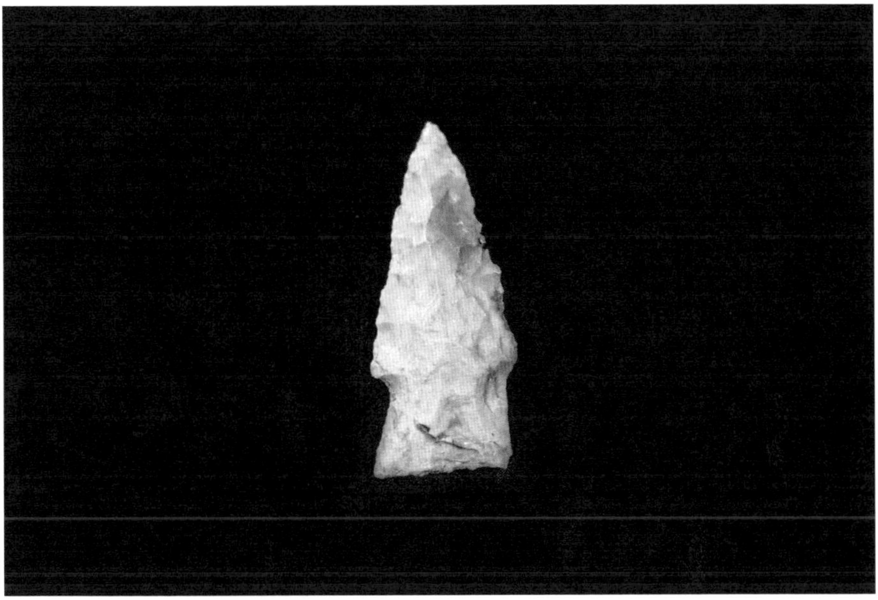

Late Woodland Period projectile point. *Courtesy of Steve Snodgress.*

Fisher and Huber populations and Oneota.[26] Sandwiched between the Fort Ancient in western Ohio and the Mississippian cultures in Illinois, the Native populations living in the west fork White River Valley appear to be diverse, sharing characteristics from "the boundaries between cultures [that were] neither fixed nor impermeable."[27]

MISSISSIPPIAN AND FORT ANCIENT CULTURES

Another Native American culture built large earthwork mounds, although for very different purposes than their Adena and Hopewell predecessors. Centered near modern-day St. Louis at Cahokia, an agricultural-based, chieftain society began to flourish, known generally as the Mississippian Culture. Starting around 900 CE and extending in some areas to the time of early European contact, Mississippian cultures built massive platform mounds across the Mississippi River Valley, lower Ohio River Valley and throughout the Southeast. These platform mounds were not only much larger, but also served different functions than Adena and Hopewell earthworks. Instead of serving religious, calendric or mortuary purposes, the Mississippian mounds often possessed chieftain

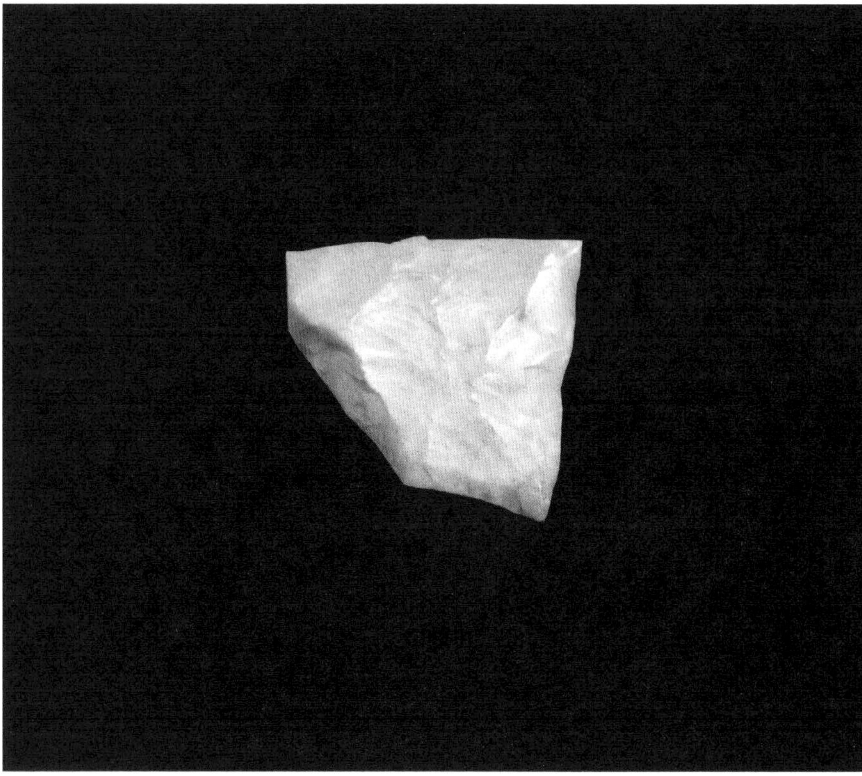

Late Mississippian, Late Pre-Contact point. *Courtesy of Josef Zacek.*

houses and other structures at their summits. In Indiana, the Angel Mounds archaeological site near Evansville contains Mississippian earthworks along the Ohio River. Mississippian cultures are also distinctive from their Adena and Hopewell forerunners by relying heavily on corn as a primary crop.[28]

Around this same time period in Ohio, the Fort Ancient Culture flourished from approximately 1000 CE to 1750 CE.[29] Centered in what is now southern Ohio and extending into Indiana, Kentucky and West Virginia, Fort Ancient peoples also constructed specialized earthworks for religious and burial purposes, with early developments of platform mounds, palisades and earthworks designed to mark the seasonal changes. Although Fort Ancient peoples relied on hunting and gathering, they continued development of domesticated farming practices. Although scholars debate the origins, the Great Serpent Mound in Adams County, Ohio, represents earthworks built or modified by Fort Ancient peoples. The effigy mound is 1,348 feet long and depicts a serpent, partly coiled, either wrapping its head around an egg or capped with an oval shape at the

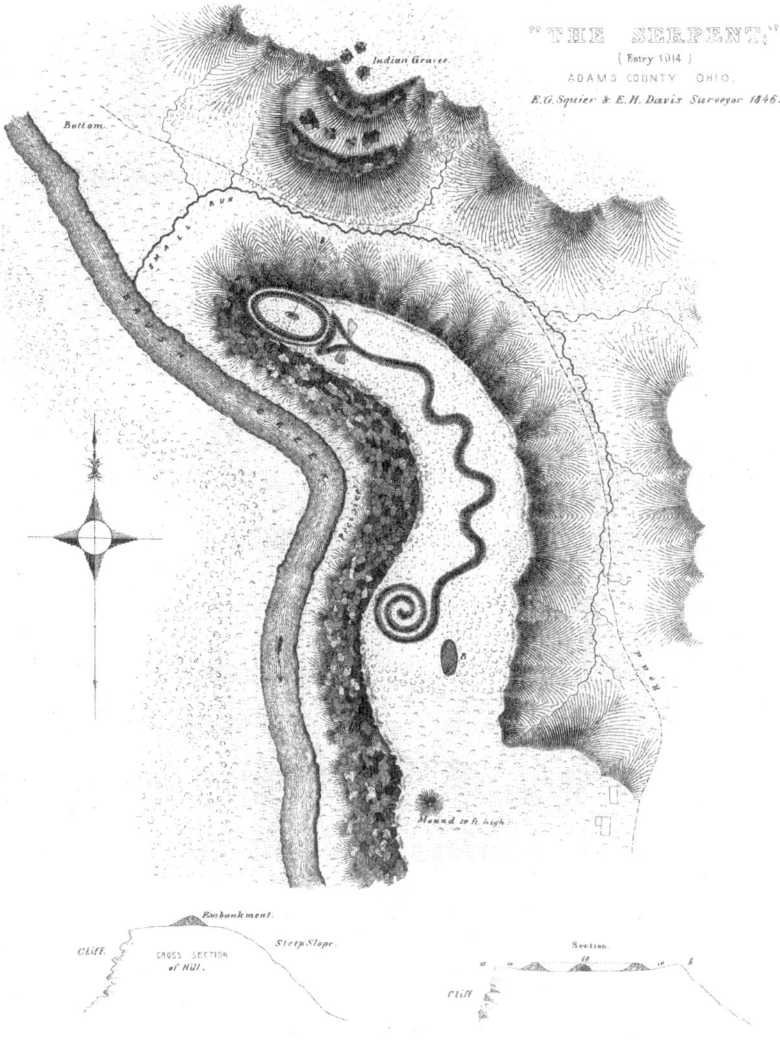

Squire and Davis's 1848 etching of the Serpent Mound. *Courtesy of Internet Archive.*

head. Archaeologists debate as to whether the signature mound was built by the Adena or Fort Ancient peoples, with carbon dating showing evidence for both.[30] Some scholars believe that the Great Serpent Mound was built by Adena and modified later by the Fort Ancient.[31]

COLLAPSE FROM DISEASE

When early settlers came across the earthworks as they moved into the Ohio country and the American Southeast,[32] they often asked the existing Shawnee, Miami and Lenape as to the origins and meaning. The tribes knew next to nothing concerning the earthworks' origins, suggesting to the settlers that they were built by a mysterious race of lost "moundbuilders." It was taken quite seriously at the time.[33] Modern scholars have confirmed beyond any sensible doubt that the earthworks, effigy mounds, mortuary mounds and enclosures in the Ohio River Valley watershed were indeed built by ancestors of post-contact Native Americans. While archaeologists continue to revise the precise dates of their findings, the exact connection between the pre-European contact "moundbuilders" and their post-contact descendants remains unknown. While some evidence suggests that the Shawnee are descendants from a Fort Ancient Culture[34] and the Miami from a Mississippian Culture,[35] archaeologists have yet to find conclusive evidence linking pre-contact groups with their post-contact successors.

However the pre- and post-contact groups connect, we do know that disease ravaged indigenous cultures for hundreds of years during European colonization. Charles C. Mann's *1491* explores what life was like in the Americas prior to Columbus's landing in the Caribbean islands. In Mann's *1493*, he explores the decades following Native American and European interaction in what is referred to as the "Columbian Exchange," or the movement of peoples, plants, animals and diseases from the Americas to the African and Eurasian continents and vice versa.[36]

Part of the exchange considered by Mann in both books involves a comprehensive evaluation of the massive population loss suffered by many indigenous cultures in North and South America after the arrival of Europeans. Mann suggests that due to the extensive trade networks on both continents, thousands of people were dying of European diseases long before Europeans ever made direct contact. Spreading from the Caribbean, Central America and the American Southeast, disease ravaged indigenous groups perhaps hundreds of years before the first white settlements. As the early European explorers wrote about pristine forests, uninhabited river valleys and small hunter-gatherer groups in the interior of the continent, their accounts probably reflect the state immediately following a massive population collapse.

Part I

Ancient Inhabitants Along the White River

Chapter 1

Pre-Contact Midwest

While it is convenient for us to discuss the history of east-central Indiana in regard to the current political map, we must remember that state boundaries are recent demarcations. The indigenous past of central and southern Indiana is a history best organized around the waterways in the Ohio River watershed. The pre-contact indigenous history is a history of the

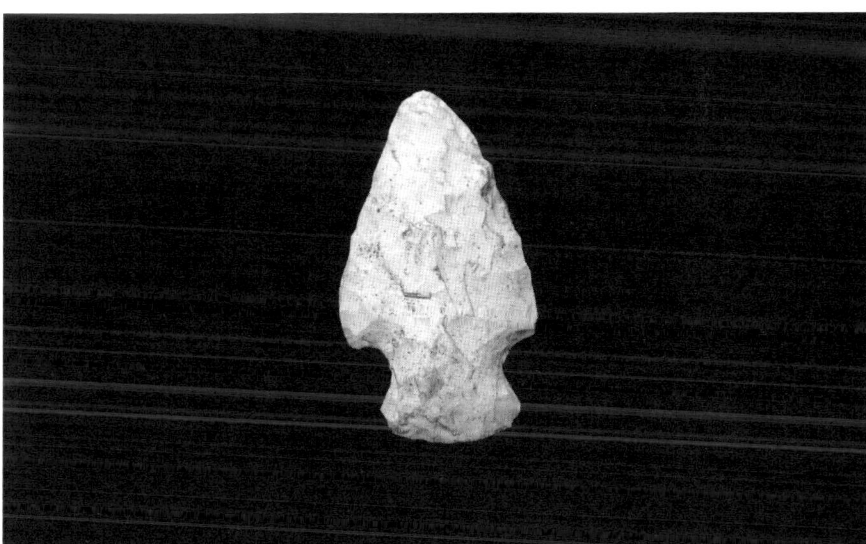

Late Archaic point. *Courtesy of Josef Zacek.*

Ohio River Valley, with the west and east forks of the White, Mississinewa, Whitewater, Great Miami, Little Miami, Scioto and Wabash Rivers as primary geographic markers. The pre-contact Native Americans in this area lived along these waterways. As the groups increased social complexity and technological evolution, they began the construction of earthworks. Most of the mounds, enclosures, village sites and other earthworks built by pre-contact peoples in east-central Indiana and the Ohio River Valley are found immediately adjacent to these waterways.[37]

WOODLAND PERIOD

While we do know that Paleoindian and Archaic peoples lived in what is now Indiana, archaeologists have yet to discover any large Paleoindian or Archaic archaeological sites in east-central Indiana.[38] However, there are thousands of smaller sites from these periods, with the possibility of more to be discovered. We simply do not have enough synthesis of the available archaeological record to fully understand and comment conclusively. In east-central Indiana, we do know that the area was inhabited prominently during the Woodland Period. Stretching from approximately 1000 BCE to 1000 CE, the Woodland Period is best "characterized by a continuing dependence on hunting, gathering, fishing, and collecting with increased reliance on the controlled production of indigenous plant foods, with widespread use of grit-tempered ceramic pottery, the development of extensive and active interregional exchange networks, and burial of the dead away from habitation sites—most notably, but certainly not always, beneath or in earthen or stone mounds."[39]

The Woodland Period is further divided into the Early Woodland Period, 1000–1 BCE; Middle Woodland Period, 1–500 CE; and the Late Woodland Period, 500–1000 CE. The Early Woodland Period is marked by the development and use of pottery around the year 1000 BCE, with an increasing number of permanent or semipermanent village sites, as well as the construction of earthworks. Archaeologists refer to the cultures in southern Ohio during this time as Adena. The Early Woodland Period also marked a transition into the domestication of plants, albeit only in a supportive role to hunting and gathering. Known as the Eastern Agricultural Complex, indigenous populations living in the Early Woodland Period cultivated goosefoot, marshelder and sunflowers.[40]

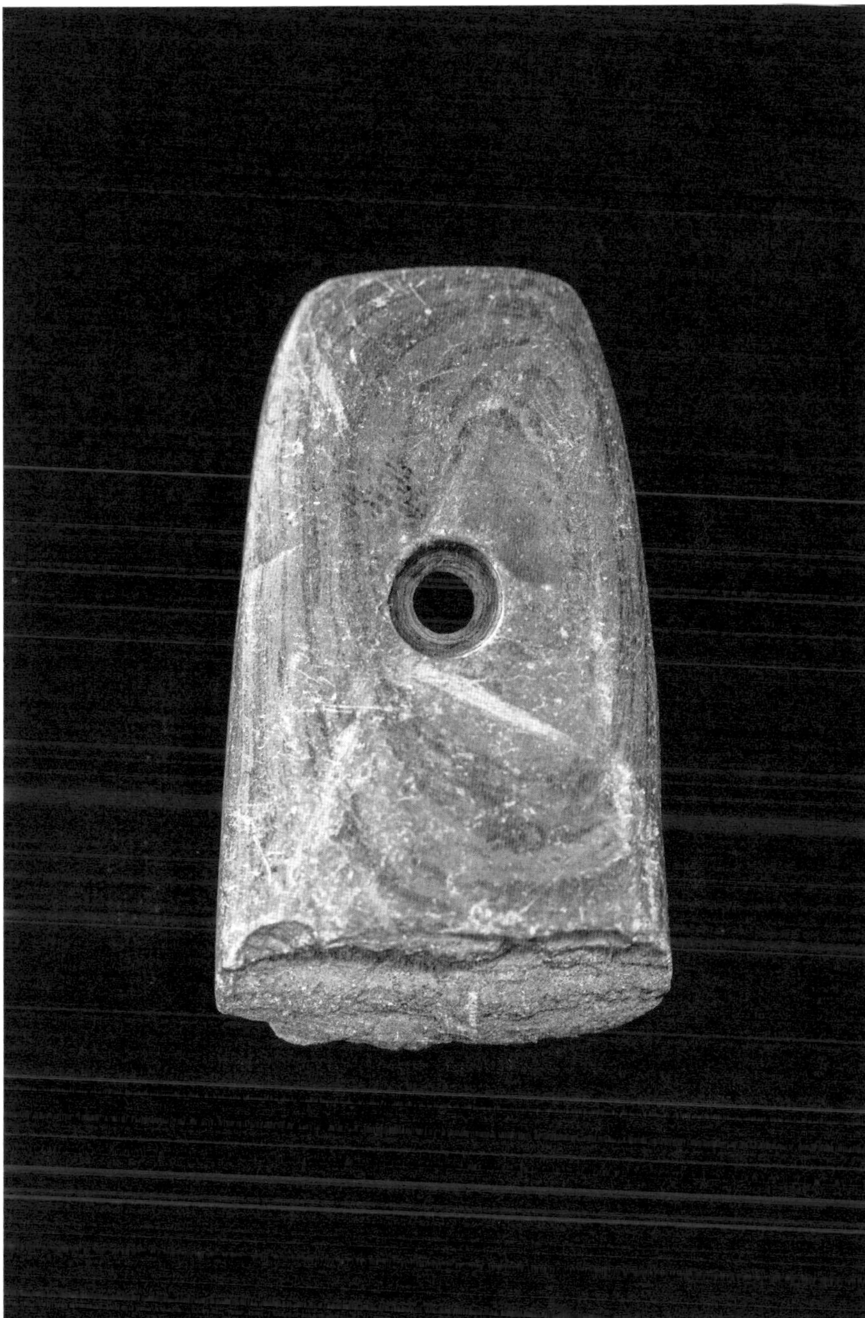

Early Woodland Period gorget. *Courtesy of Steve Snodgress.*

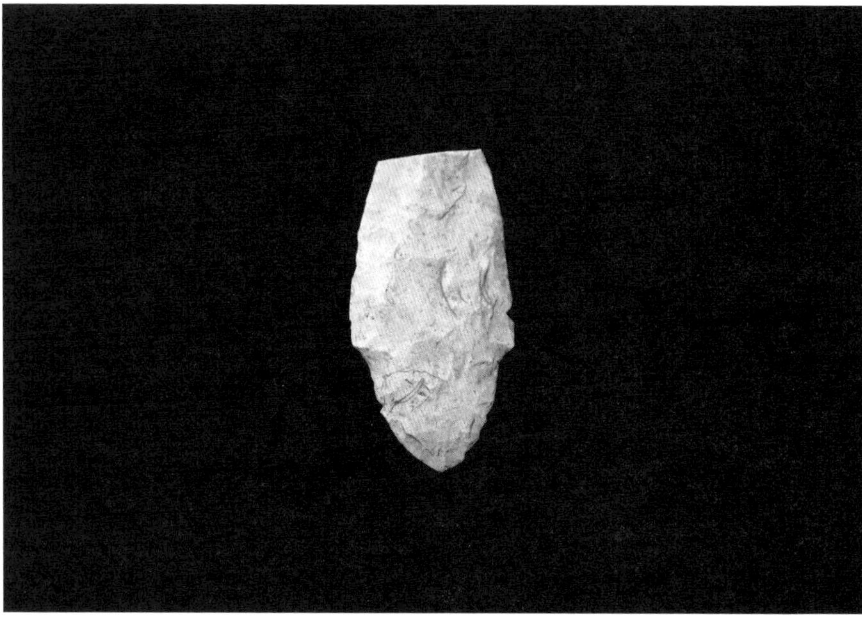

Adena Point (Early Woodland). *Courtesy of Helen Zacek.*

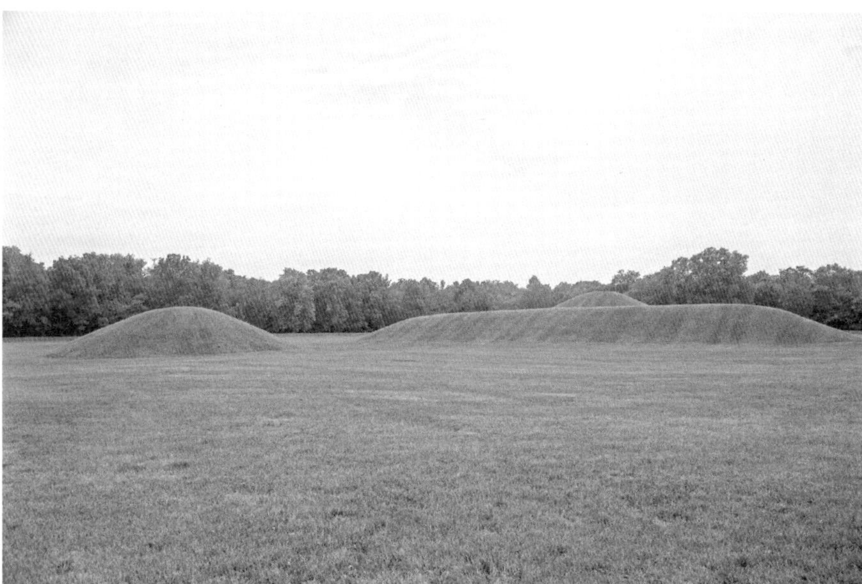

Hopewell Culture National Historical Park, the heart of Ohio Hopewell activity. *Author's collection.*

The Eastern Agricultural Complex is a remarkable development, as it represents one of a few regions on the planet where humans developed agricultural food production independently.[11]

During the Middle Woodland Period, the cultures in the Ohio River watershed continued their experimentation with plant domestication, earthwork construction and the development of a complex exchange network of manufactured goods. In the Ohio River watershed, archaeologists refer to the indigenous groups in the Middle Woodland Period as Classic Hopewell, or Ohio Hopewell. The Ohio Hopewell's most extravagant artifacts and earthworks were discovered in the Scioto River Valley. Along with earthworks, the Ohio Hopewell were part of a large Hopewell exchange network, known as the Hopewell Interaction Sphere, with other groups in North America. The Hopewell Interaction Sphere included the exchange of exotic goods across North America from what is now Canada to the Gulf of Mexico. Other Hopewell groups existed alongside the Ohio Hopewell, including the Crab Orchard Culture, Havana Hopewell, Marksville Culture, Swift Creek Culture, Laurel Complex and the New York Hopewell.

During the Late Woodland Period, the Hopewell Interaction Sphere ceased to function, along with the elaborate mound building in the Ohio River watershed. Indigenous groups began using bow and arrows, and the domestication of plants included an increased use of squash, beans and corn. In *Late Woodland Societies: Traditions and Transformations Across the Midcontinent*,[42] the authors conclude that three transformations took place during the Late Woodland Period: a breakdown of the interaction sphere and a "Balkanization" of societies after 300–400 BCE,[43] the adoption of the bow and arrow to replace the spear and atlatl and the adoption of corn. During this period, indigenous groups began geographically ubiquitous agriculture with "nucleated" villages.[44]

Adena

The most prominent group with an identifiable archaeological record in southern Ohio and east-central Indiana during the Early Woodland Period is commonly referred to as Adena and existed from approximately 1000 BCE to 200 BCE. Although the use of "Adena" is not entirely accepted among all archaeologists,[45] east-central Indiana archaeologists Beth McCord and Donald Cochran concluded that "the idea of an Adena identity remains firmly fixed in the collective mind of Midwestern archaeologists."[46] While some find the term imprecise, it is useful in identifying the people sharing the same cultural characteristics in the Ohio River watershed during the Early Woodland Period. The archaeologist Brian Fagan views Adena as "a convenient archaeological term that covers dozens of local Early and sometimes Middle Woodland cultures that were contemporary, often close neighbors, and interacted with one another continuously."[47]

The Adena archaeological record includes various earthworks and other artifacts, including "[a] tubular pipe style, mica cutouts, copper bracelets and cutouts, incised tablets, stemmed projectile points, oval bifaces, concave and reel-shaped gorgets, and thick ceramic vessels decorated with incised geometric designs."[48] The earthworks include non-burial circular enclosures[49] and conical mounds, often with human remains. The burial mounds were "the very essence of the Adena."[50] The mounds were most likely used for burial of honored dead, with the other enclosures serving ceremonial purposes, perhaps even territorial markers. We know little about the Adena village sites[51] and, therefore, know little about the domesticated life of these peoples beyond their hunting, gathering and small-scale domestication of a few plants consistent with the beginnings of the Eastern Agricultural Complex.

Fagan further defined the Adena as possessing "a series of mortuary rituals and spiritual beliefs that have come down to us in the form of hundreds of burial mounds"[52] and noted that the Adena had a variety of burial customs, where they essentially were "a large number of interacting societies that drew upon a common repertoire of mortuary practices, symbols, and ideas."[53] In some mounds, the Adena would place their dead in small pits at the floor and cover the pit with bark. In other mounds, the Adena would build a "charnel house" with a roof, where the dead would be placed inside and then covered with a conical mound. Other burial mounds were more elaborate, "built with large logs lining the sides and floor, and making up the roof. The mourners often sprinkled the dead with powdered red ocher…Grieving relatives occasionally painted the corpse with red ochre paint as well."[54] The Adena are also known for their "sacred circles" that are often less than five hundred feet in diameter.[55] We do not know much about the circles' cultural functions. Many of the ceremonial circles were identical and "perfectly circular and surrounded by a ditch with the dirt thrown outside."[56] Other Adena sites include circular post structures and large ditched villages.[57]

Like the later Ohio Hopewell, the Adena culture seems to have been centered on the Scioto River Valley, south of modern-day Chillicothe,

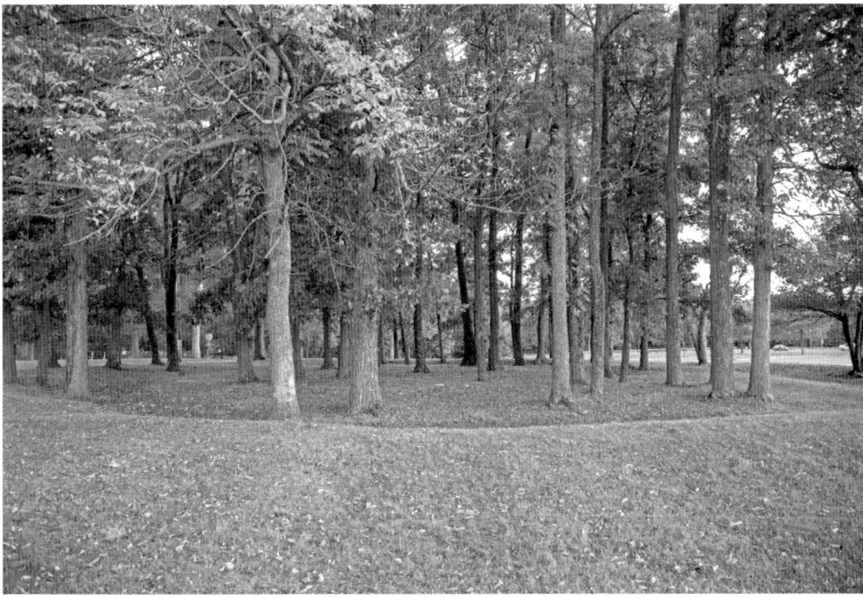

Isolated enclosure or "sacred circle" in New Castle. *Courtesy of Jarred Scott.*

Ohio, and a second concentration around the Kanawaha River Valley in Charleston, West Virginia.[58] The Adena had other, albeit smaller population centers in Indiana and Kentucky.[59] The Adena mounds and enclosures found in east-central Indiana are discussed in the next chapter.

Ohio Hopewell

Ohio Hopewell flourished throughout the Middle Woodland Period, with their primary center in south-central Ohio in the Scioto River Valley. The term "Hopewell," like "Adena," is not universally accepted among all scholars and "is an entirely nonanalytic term and represents a relic of an earlier age in archaeological thought."[60] However, "it is no less informative as a heuristic device as are comparably vague terms such as Early Woodland or Late Prehistoric."[61] The term "Ohio Hopewell" covers a variety of peoples living across the Ohio River watershed, "but there was nonetheless sufficient interaction and sharing of a common world view to allow the composite population to interact regularly, effectively, and constructively."[62] We refer to many different populations of those living in this area during the Middle Woodland Period as Ohio

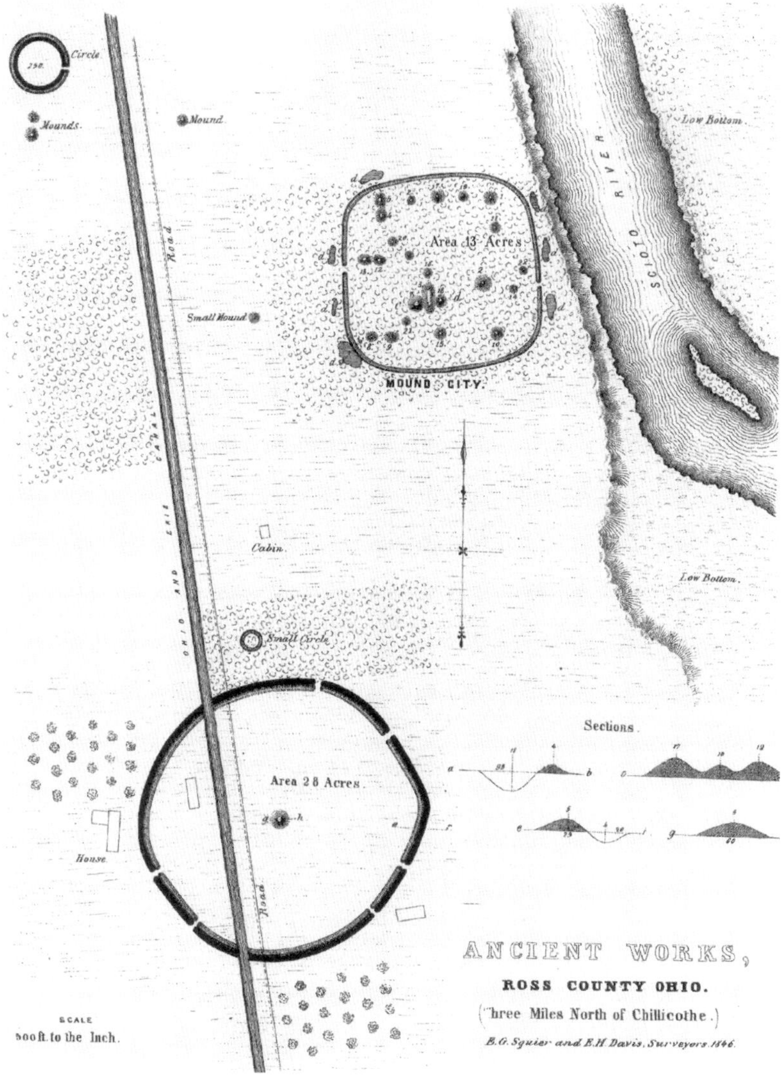

Squire and Davis's early map of the "Mound City" archaeological site. *Courtesy of Internet Archive.*

Hopewell. While Hopewellian traits are found in peoples all across the eastern United States, two prominent concentration centers of Hopewellian culture existed in Illinois and Ohio along the Scioto River.[63] The Hopewellian remains found in east-central Indiana were similar to the Ohio Hopewell. The Ohio Hopewell built large earthworks and mounds and crafted fantastic artifacts, often from rare materials. They flourished from approximately 200 BCE until 400 CE and probably lived at the same time as some Adena populations.

Like many pre-contact indigenous cultures, we can only interpret a way of life based on the material evidence left behind. The Ohio Hopewell continued the practice of domesticating plants such as goosefoot, squash, maygrass and corn to support hunting and gathering. Due to the extensive interaction sphere, the Ohio Hopewell had access to exotic materials with which they crafted exquisite artifacts. Recovered artifacts include elaborate stone tobacco pipes, mica figurines, shell beads, stamped pottery and flint projectile points. Items such as alligator teeth and conch shells, originating probably from the Gulf of Mexico, have been found in the Scioto River Valley, suggesting a large exchange network.

This "exchange network" involved indigenous peoples exchanging materials across what is now the eastern United States. It is called an interaction sphere or exchange network because archaeologists have no evidence to suggest a trade network in the modern sense of exchanging goods. The Ohio Hopewell were the eastern core of the Hopewell Interaction Sphere, and the Havana Hopewell, centered on the Mississippi and Illinois Rivers in modern-day Illinois, were at the western core. The Havana Hopewell and Ohio Hopewell are located "at the center of a large, interregional network. In time, they overlapped with one another, but they never lost their own identities."[64] East-central Indiana was therefore in the middle of the two Hopewell centers. The exchange network extended down to the Gulf of Mexico and north to the Great Lakes.

The most prominent feature in Ohio Hopewell archaeology includes the earthwork mounds and enclosures, the greatest concentration of which lie in the Scioto River Valley, south of Chillicothe, Ohio. Archaeologists differ in their understandings about how the Ohio Hopewell lived and if they lived near the earthworks.[65] Popular among some archaeologists is a living pattern referred to as the Dispersed Sedentary Community model, developed by Paul Pacheco and William Dancey.[66] The Dispersed Sedentary Community model suggests that the mounds served ritualistic functions, where "Hopewellian communities being made up of single- or multiple-family households scattered across the landscape but concentrated around the centrally located burial and ceremonial precincts."[67] With this model of understanding, the Ohio Hopewell lived in small family-based units near earthworks, but not immediately adjacent to them. During specified times of year, the Ohio Hopewell would gather at the earthworks to conduct religious or cultural ceremonies. In addition to mounds, the

Ohio Hopewell constructed geometric enclosures, hilltop enclosures and circular earthworks.[68]

While it would take thousands of pages to describe, define and discuss the varying interpretations concerning the various Ohio Hopewell earthworks, a few patterns emerge from the literature. The mounds were often burials for high-status individuals who were laid "in log-lined tombs within the charnel houses, accompanied by a diverse array of artifacts."[69] Charnel houses were ceremonial structures built to prepare the dead for the afterlife. Once the ceremony was completed, earth was piled on top of the body, perhaps over many generations until a prominent mound was formed. Buried with the dead, "mourners deposited copper axes, cut-out silhouettes of birds, fish, claws, and human heads and hands in copper or mica, flint and chlorite disks, finely polished stone atlatl weights, and beautiful effigy pipes."[70] We know little about the utility of the non-mortuary earthworks. Archaeologists suspect that "some and perhaps all of the lowland sites that developed earthwork complexes fulfilled multiple corporate functions and probably, with time and the development of tradition, assumed expanded symbolic importance."[71]

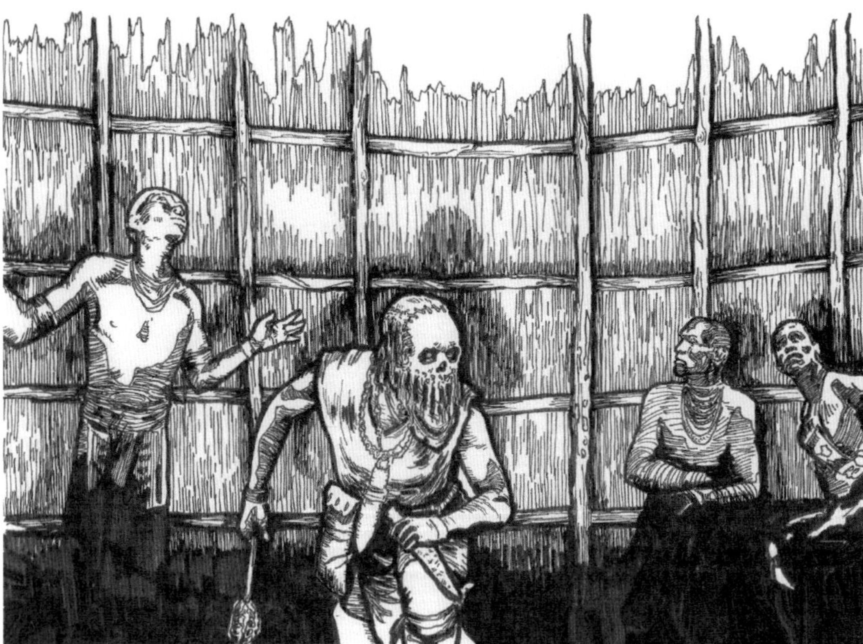

An artist's rendering of a Hopewell religious ceremony. Image inspired by Romain's *Shamans of the Lost World* and a headdress found at Mound City. *Courtesy of George Everett Keller.*

Perhaps we may never fully understand the Adena's or Ohio Hopewell's use of the earthworks, nor their specific ways of life. With so many of mounds and enclosures having been destroyed by early settlers' agricultural practices, it might never be possible to fully ascertain the complexity of these peoples. Perhaps new evidence will present itself in the ensuing decades, with revelations and interpretations gleaned from new evidence still buried.

Chapter 2

Early and Middle Woodland Native Americans

In Randolph County, the west fork of the White River begins as a small creek, winding around farms, villages and hamlets before starting a westerly direction through Winchester, flowing just south of Farmland, Parker City and Selma. The White cuts through east-central Indiana's main river towns, Muncie, Yorktown, Daleville, Chesterfield and Anderson. The river continues west until it passes north of Strawtown, turning sharply south, flowing into Noblesville and then into Indianapolis before continuing southwest to the Wabash River. Archaeologists have found numerous Woodland Period remains along this waterway.

This pre-contact evidence in east-central Indiana is unique and does not precisely match as Adena and Ohio Hopewell remains. Archaeologists Beth McCord and Donald Cochran specifically studied the indigenous groups in east-central Indiana during the Early and Middle Woodland Periods. Although related, they found in the archaeological record a unique complexity of artifacts that did not clearly fit into Adena and Hopewell categories, suggesting that in east-central Indiana, the "Adena and Hopewell were two different components of the same contemporaneous ceremonial system."[72]

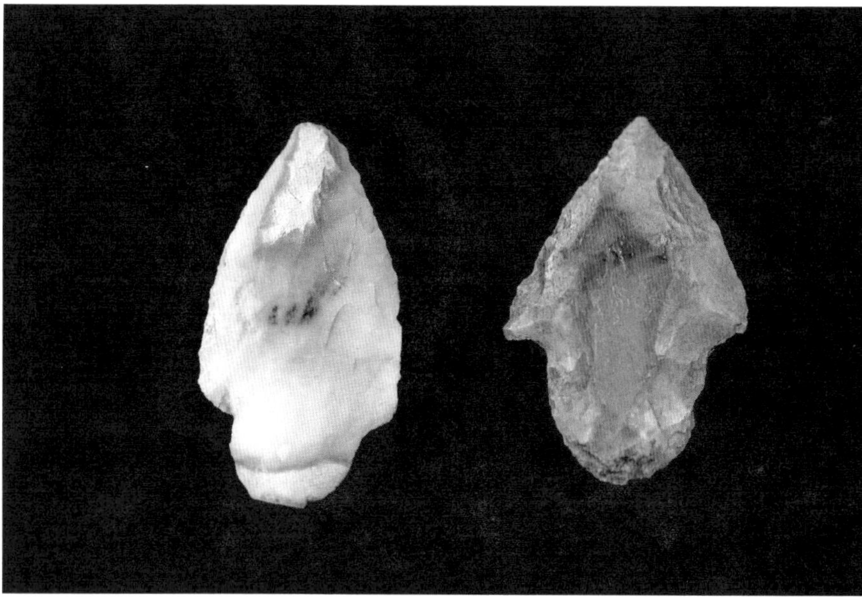

Early Woodland Period projectile point. *Courtesy of Steve Snodgress.*

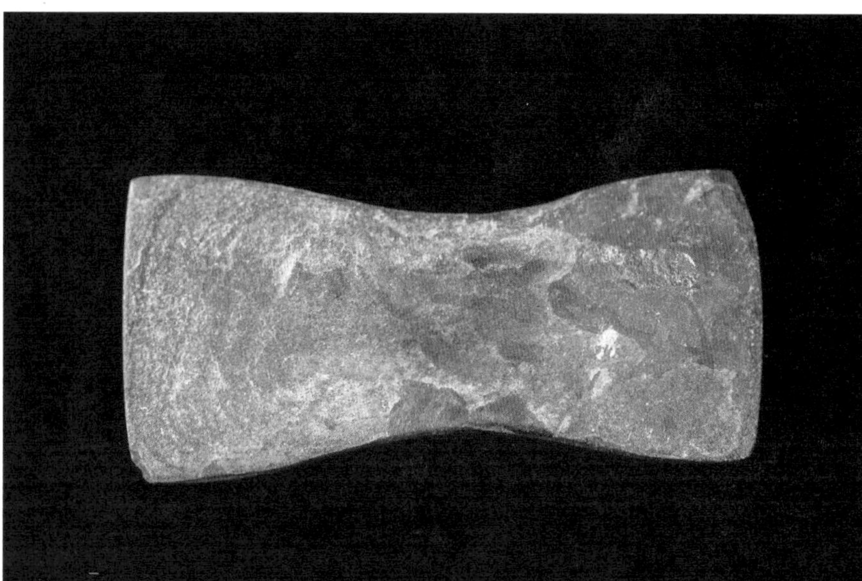

Eastern Woodland Period gorget. *Courtesy of Steve Snodgress.*

NEW CASTLE PHASE NATIVE AMERICANS

McCord and Cochran revived[73] the New Castle Phase term to describe the mound and earthwork building indigenous populations in east-central Indiana during the Early and Middle Woodland Periods that exhibited both Adena and Ohio Hopewell characteristics.[74] The New Castle Phase Native Americans existed from approximately 250 BCE until 350 CE. In McCord's and Cochran's 2006 *The Fudge Site: A New Look at an Ancient Monument, Randolph County*, they identified the geographic boundary, earthwork sites and artifact record of the New Castle Phase Native Americans. Geographically, New Castle Phase inhabitants lived along the waterways in Randolph, Delaware, Madison, Henry and Wayne Counties, near the west and east forks of the White River and subsequent tributaries, as well as the watershed areas of the Whitewater River. While not all pre-contact archaeological sites in east-central Indiana are considered part of the New Castle Phase, the researchers have found that "[a]pproximately 100 mounds and earthworks are reported in east-central Indiana but most have been heavily disturbed or destroyed."[75] Archaeologists only have excavation data from twelve of these sites.[76] The New Castle Phase archaeological sites include earthwork enclosures and mounds. The specific New Castle Phase sites include "the Anderson

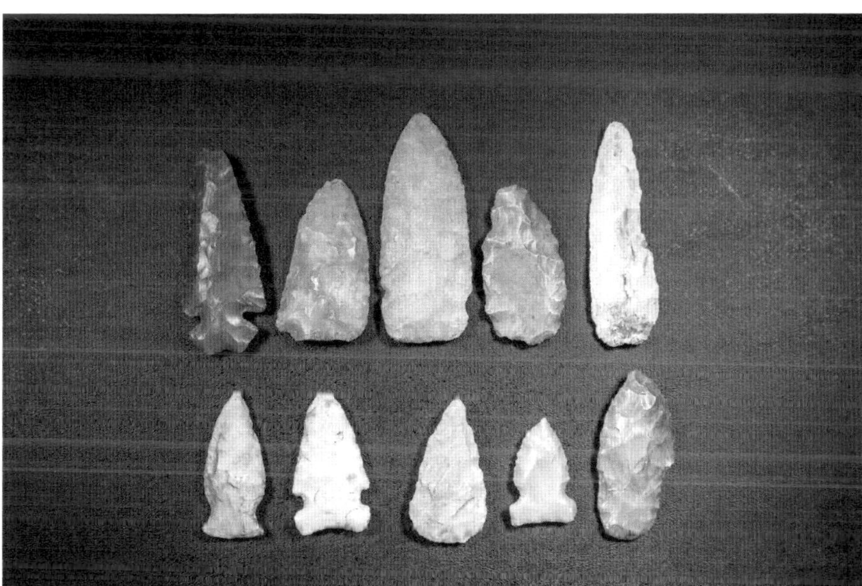

Collection of projectile points found in Indiana. *Courtesy of Alan Flook.*

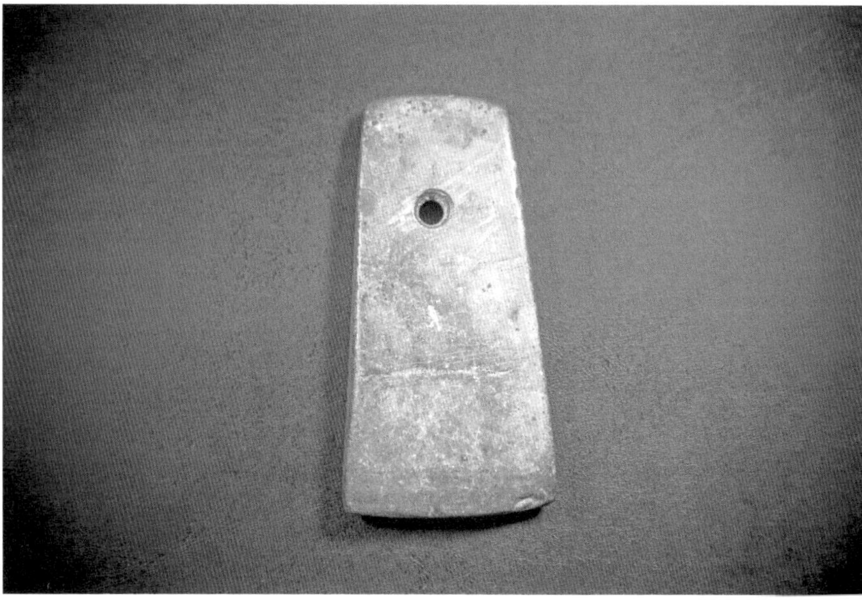

Gorget found in central Indiana. *Courtesy of Alan Flook.*

complex, the New Castle complex, the Bertsch complex, the Fudge site, the Graves site, Wolford Mound, Windsor Mound, Law Mound, the White site, Waterworks Mound, Hayes Arboretum Mound and the Chrysler Enclosure…Other sites that likely belong to the phase include Johnson Mound, Baxter Mound, Bell Creek Mound and Parkinson Mound."[77] Following the publication of the *Fudge Site*, a new enclosure was discovered in Yorktown, and while it has not been thoroughly excavated, it generally fits with New Castle Phase earthworks. These sites are scattered all across east-central Indiana in farm fields and residential areas along waterways.

The recovered artifacts from many of these sites, while varying from location to location, seem to suggest "a regionally distinct group,"[78] with the following items found: Adena projectile points, sandstone tablets, bar gorgets, pipes, fake bear teeth, beads, awls, breastplates, pearls, conch shells, objects made from mica and ceramics.[79]

Mounds, Enclosures and Earthworks

The most visible remnants found today from the New Castle Phase are the mounds, enclosures and earthworks left behind in their "ceremonial landscape"[80] in east-central Indiana. While we many never fully understand the purpose of the earthworks, archaeologists have concluded several characteristics exclusive to east-central Indiana,[81] including that the construction and use of the earthworks occurred at the same time; the earthworks locations were not accidental; the known enclosure complexes split east-central Indiana into five or six different parts; the known circular and rectangular complexes split east-central Indiana into two parts; earthwork locations were sites of unique activities; the burial and other ceremonial mounds are approximately halfway between the rectangular earthwork complexes; the traditionally identified Adena and Hopewell recovered artifacts are actually part of one ceremonial system; and, most amazingly, the earthworks "are organized in relation to astronomical events."[82]

The latter characteristic is one of the more fascinating features from the New Castle Phase. If the interpretation by the archaeologists is accurate, it suggests that along with burial ceremonialism, the earthworks were designed to mark astronomical events and seasonal transitions by aligning the

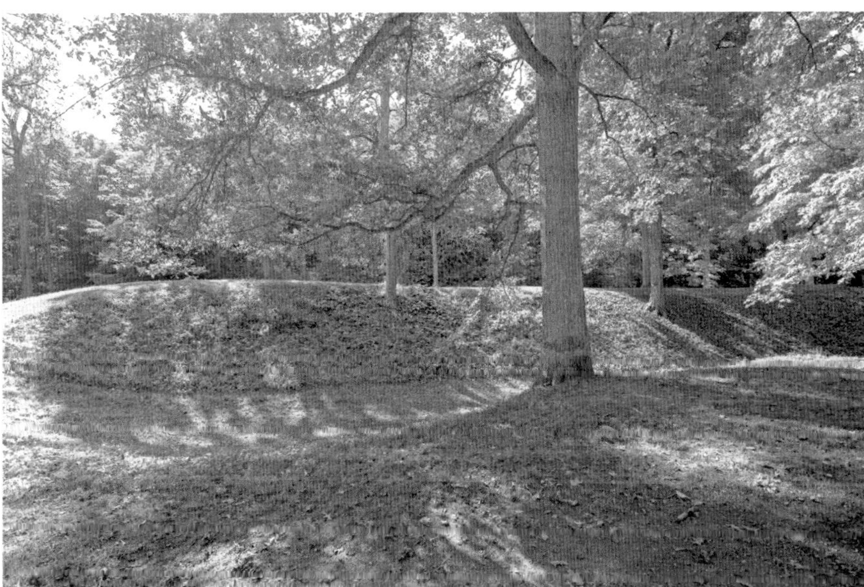

Part of the Great Mound Enclosure at Mounds State Park in Anderson. *Author's collection.*

earthworks with equinoxes and solstices. McCord and Cochran believe that "that rectangles [rectangular enclosures] equal summer and circles [circular enclosures] equate to winter…we reasoned, an association between sunset in the south at the winter solstice and the distribution of circular enclosures relates to the sunset at the north at the summer solstice and the distribution of rectangular enclosures in the region."[83] This suggests that the earthworks played a specific function for the New Castle Phase peoples, where "we can envision a regional landscape divided between enclosure complexes representing summer and winter."[84]

Earthworks in East-Central Indiana

One of the most impressive collections of earthworks in the area, still in existence today, dates from the New Castle Phase and are found at Mounds State Park in Anderson. Situated on the east side of the White River, Mounds State Park is home to circular and rectangular earthworks and mounds. Pre-contact evidence at the park dates to a time far older than the New Castle Phase, with evidence suggesting human activity extending back ten thousand years.[85] Archaeologists know of eight different circular earthworks, with four still in existence in the early twenty-first century, and two mounds that represent[86] "2 earthwork complexes, a southern group characterized by circular features and a northern group characterized by rectangular features."[87] The four circular enclosures are known as "the Great Mound enclosure, the Fiddleback enclosure, and two small circular enclosures."[88] The Great Mound enclosure is the most prominent and famous of the four and probably the most notable earthwork structure in the entire park, if not all of east-central Indiana. The Great Mound circular enclosure is approximately 350 feet wide with a 60-foot-wide ditch that is 10 feet deep.[89]

The initial construction probably began around 250 BCE and continued until 50 CE, with sporadic use thereafter.[90] During the initial construction, Native Americans placed a circular clay floor at the center of the mound and erected eighteen upright posts along north, west and east sides of the structure. At a later time, the posts were burned, and several other clay floors were placed over the first floor. Dirt was piled on top of all of this to create the general shape of the mound. About three hundred years later, a log tomb was built near the primary mound, and two bodies were buried within it.[91] While it is hard to imagine with the numerous trees surrounding

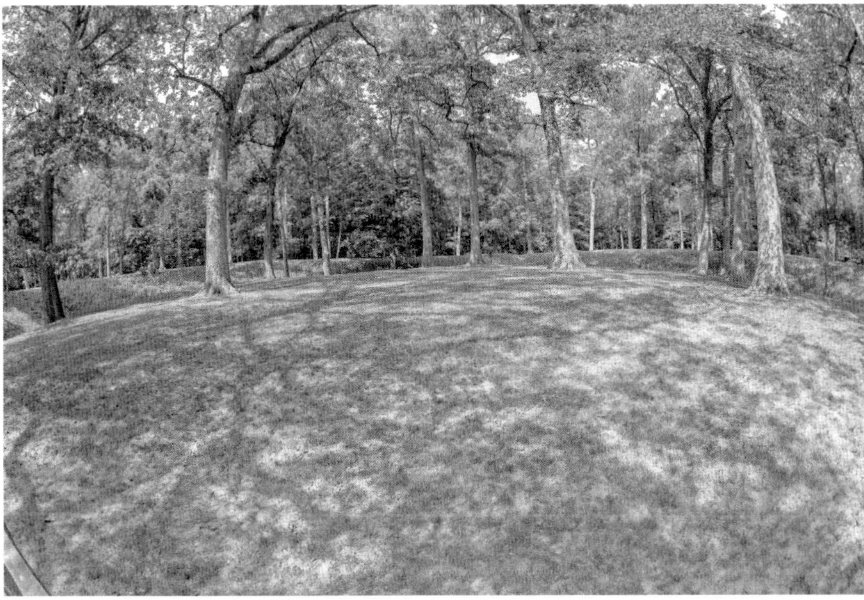

Part of the Great Mound Circular Enclosure at Mounds State Park in Anderson. *Author's collection.*

the earthwork today, Cochran and McCord believed that the structure, in part, was designed to align with astronomical events "such as the rising and setting points of some bright starts and the Pleiades in addition to serving as markers for the setting sun at the winter and summer solstices and equinoxes. Confirmation of some of these alignments occur between earthworks in the southern complex while Circle Mound is laid out to record the solar alignments."[92] While we may never fully understand the utility of these structures, "The presence of astronomical alignments supports the idea that the site was used, at least in part, for astronomically based calendric purposes, perhaps as a way to schedule major ritual activities at the site."[93] Whatever the purpose, the Great Mound and surrounding earthworks at Mounds State Park are impressive to say the least, and being located in a public park, their exploration is easy.

Near Winchester, another prominent New Castle Phase site exists in what appears as a nondescript farm field and is known as the "Fudge site." Although farming over the years has heavily disturbed the Fudge site, it remains "the largest earthen enclosure recorded in Indiana."[94] If you were to drive or walk past the site, it would not stand out more than any other farm field in Indiana. However, "the site originally consisted of a large rectangular

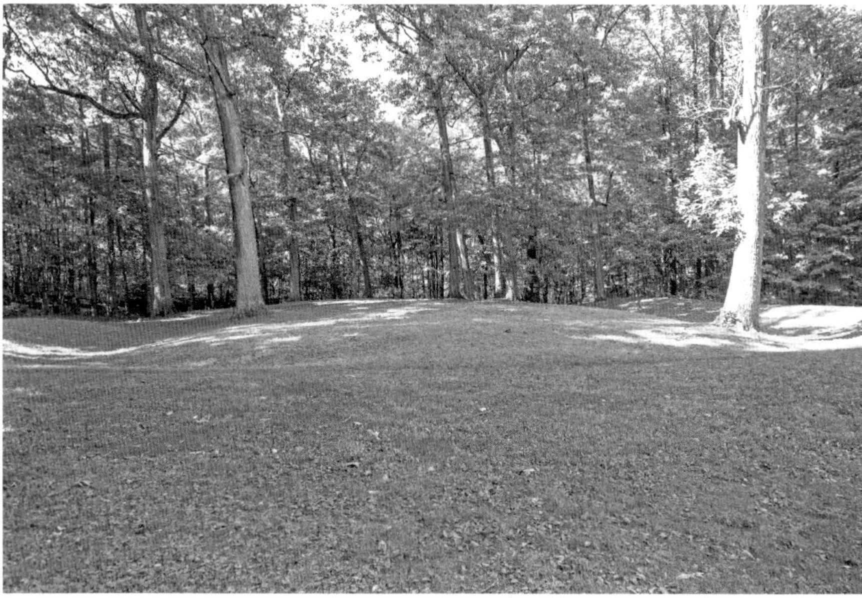

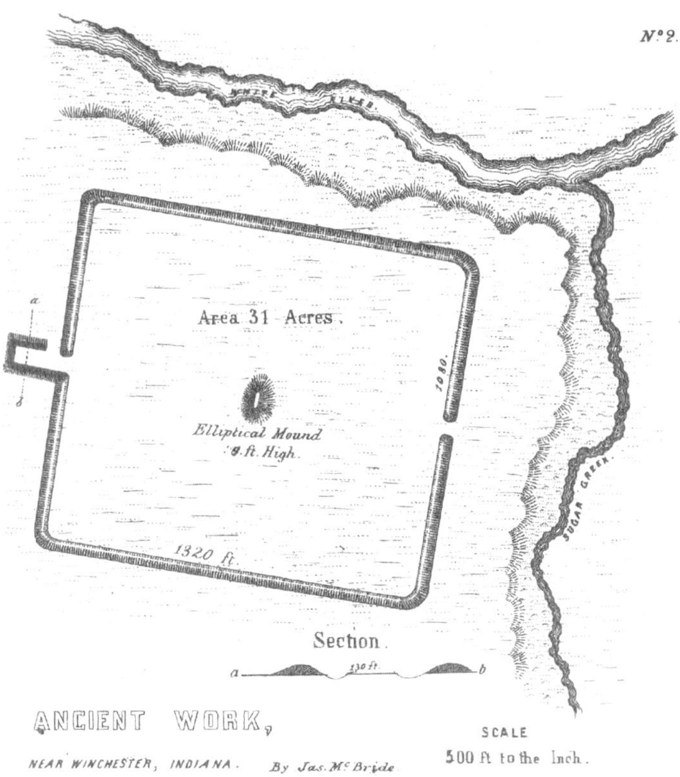

Above: Fiddleback Enclosure at Mounds State Park in Anderson. *Author's collection.*

Left: James McBride's rendering of the Fudge Earthworks in Squire and Davis's 1848 *Ancient Monuments of the Ohio Valley*.

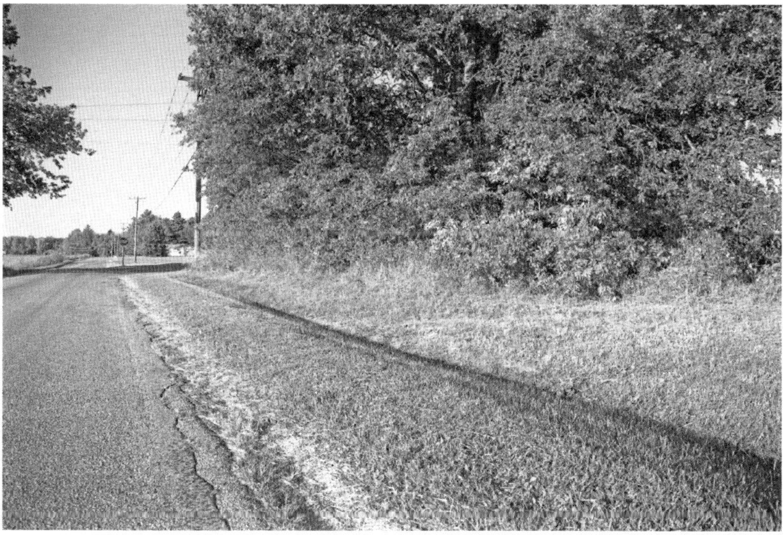

Remnants of the Fudge site's northwest earthwork enclosure. *Author's collection.*

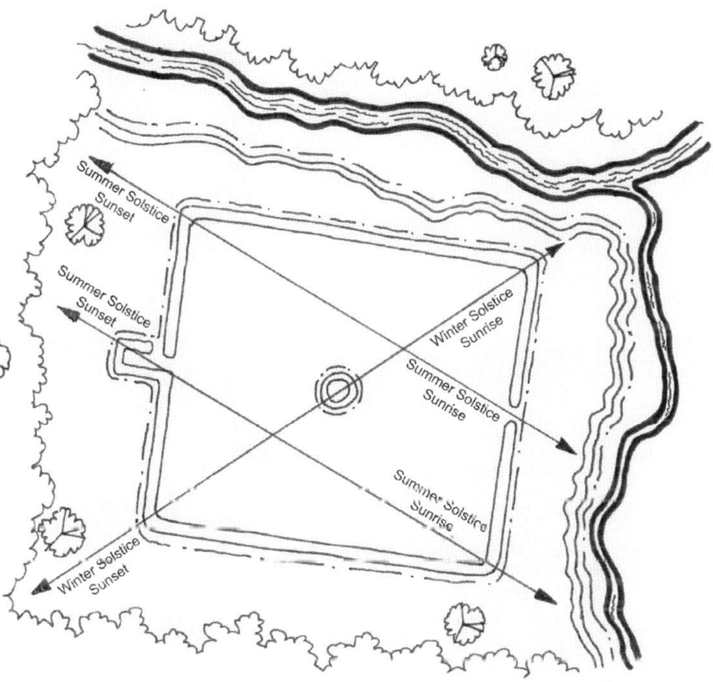

A rendering of the Fudge site. Map derived from McCord and Cochran's 2006 *Fudge Site. Courtesy of George Everett Keller.*

earth enclosure surrounding 31 to 43 acres [and] an elliptical mound 100' in diameter and 8' to 15' high was in the center of the enclosure."[95] McCord and Cochran's study of the Fudge site concluded that the recovered artifacts date[96] "between 100 [CE] and 200 [CE]...this may be the time of greatest fluorescence and expression of the Adena and Hopewell complex in the region."[97] Regarding activities at the site, the archaeologists concluded that along with mortuary activities, the Fudge site's construction included markers for sunrise and sunset, "documented through the corners of the enclosure, [and] the mound and gateways at the summer and winter solstices were confirmed."[98]

Another large earthwork complex lies southwest of the Fudge site near the city of New Castle, Indiana. The New Castle Complex site was used during historic times as an epileptic village. The construction of the facility resulted in damaging the original earthworks. Early descriptions are inconsistent,[99] but generally, the New Castle Complex features several burial mounds and about thirteen known earthworks, including circular enclosures of varying sizes.[100] Excavations at the New Castle Complex over the years suggest that the site shows a tremendous amount of complexity, with the largest diversity of known earthworks in all of east-central Indiana.[101]

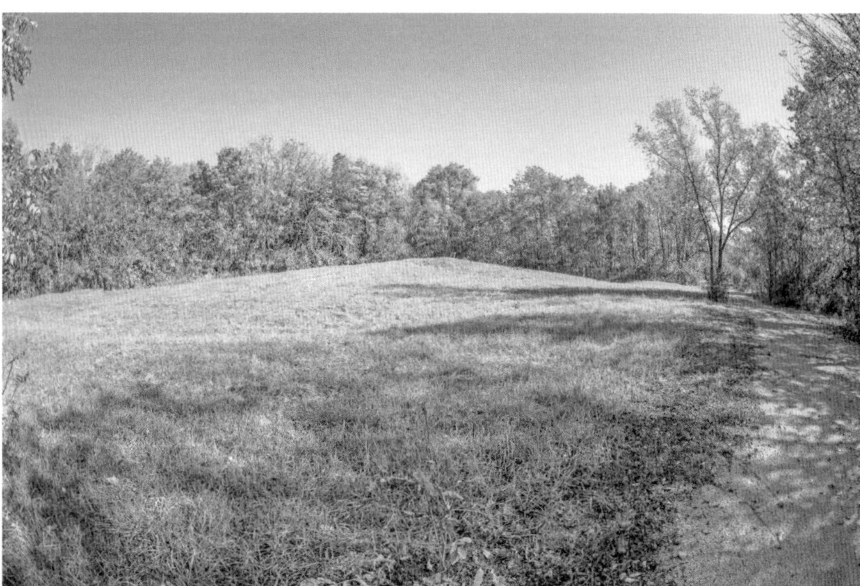

Archaeologists named the "New Castle Phase" Native Americans after evidence found at this site. *Author's collection.*

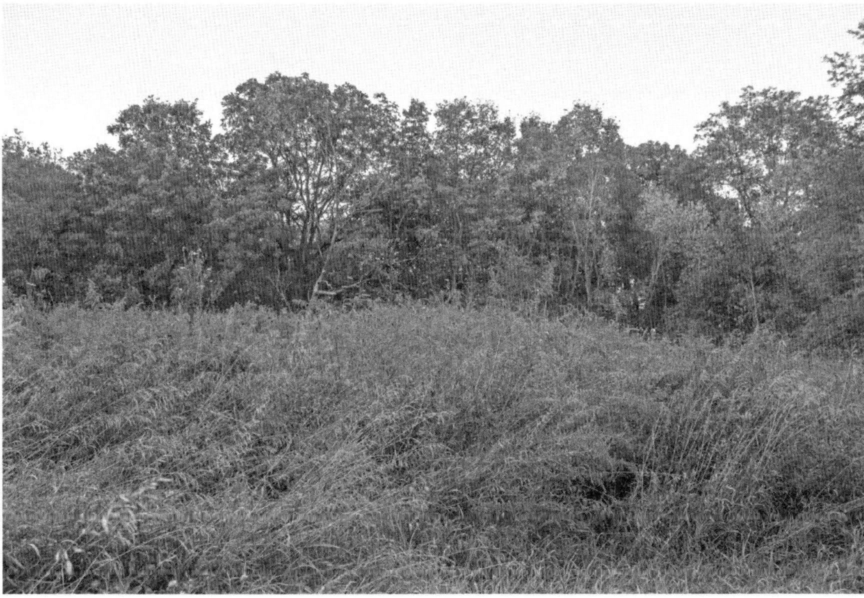

Overgrown mound at the New Castle Complex archaeological site. *Courtesy of Jarred Scott.*

A comprehensive analysis of each of the earthworks in east-central Indiana has never been done and is beyond what can be covered in this book. However, as the archaeological evidence shows, the pre-contact Early and Middle Woodland Native Americans were active in east-central Indiana. While we may never know specific details of how the New Castle Phase Native Americans lived, archaeologists glean several main characteristics from the available record. Any new evidence will, of course, modify our understanding of this mysterious indigenous period in Indiana, but generally, New Castle Phase Native Americans featured characteristics of both Adena and Hopewell from neighboring regions and were expressed variably through time and over space. More work is needed to piece together the relationship of New Castle Phase with better-known expressions of Woodland Period ceremonialism in adjacent regions.

Chapter 3

The Late Woodland Period

Evidence of Late Woodland Native Americans ceremonial and mortuary sites in east-central Indiana are not well documented nor understood; several cultures are likely to have existed, including the Intrusive Mound Culture, Albee Phase and Newtown Cultures.[102] The Intrusive Mound Culture reflects larger Late Woodland traditions in the Ohio River Valley area. Similar to other Ohio Hopewell characteristics, "These late Woodland hunting, gathering, and collecting people possessed some cultural traits that were similar to Hopewell, such as the production and use of finely crafted platform pipes, participation in interregional exchange, and funerary ritual that included the use of burial mounds."[103] The Intrusive Mound Culture is called as such due to their practice of burying their dead within existing Adena and Ohio Hopewell earthworks, along with building smaller burial mounds from time to time.[104]

In east-central Indiana, "Intrusive Mound burials have been found at Windsor, Anderson, and New Castle sites,"[105] with associated buried artifacts that include "Jack's Reef points, shell and pearl beads, a pendent, antler drifts, antler tines, bone scrapers, bone needles, beaver incisors and turtle carapace."[106] The prominence of ceremonial artifacts and earthwork complexes characteristic of Early and Middle Woodland cultures appears throughout the region in the archaeological record, with no prominent earthworks from the Late Woodland traditions.[107] However, the opposite is the case in regard to habitation sites. While we have few habitation archaeological sites for Early and Middle Woodland Periods,

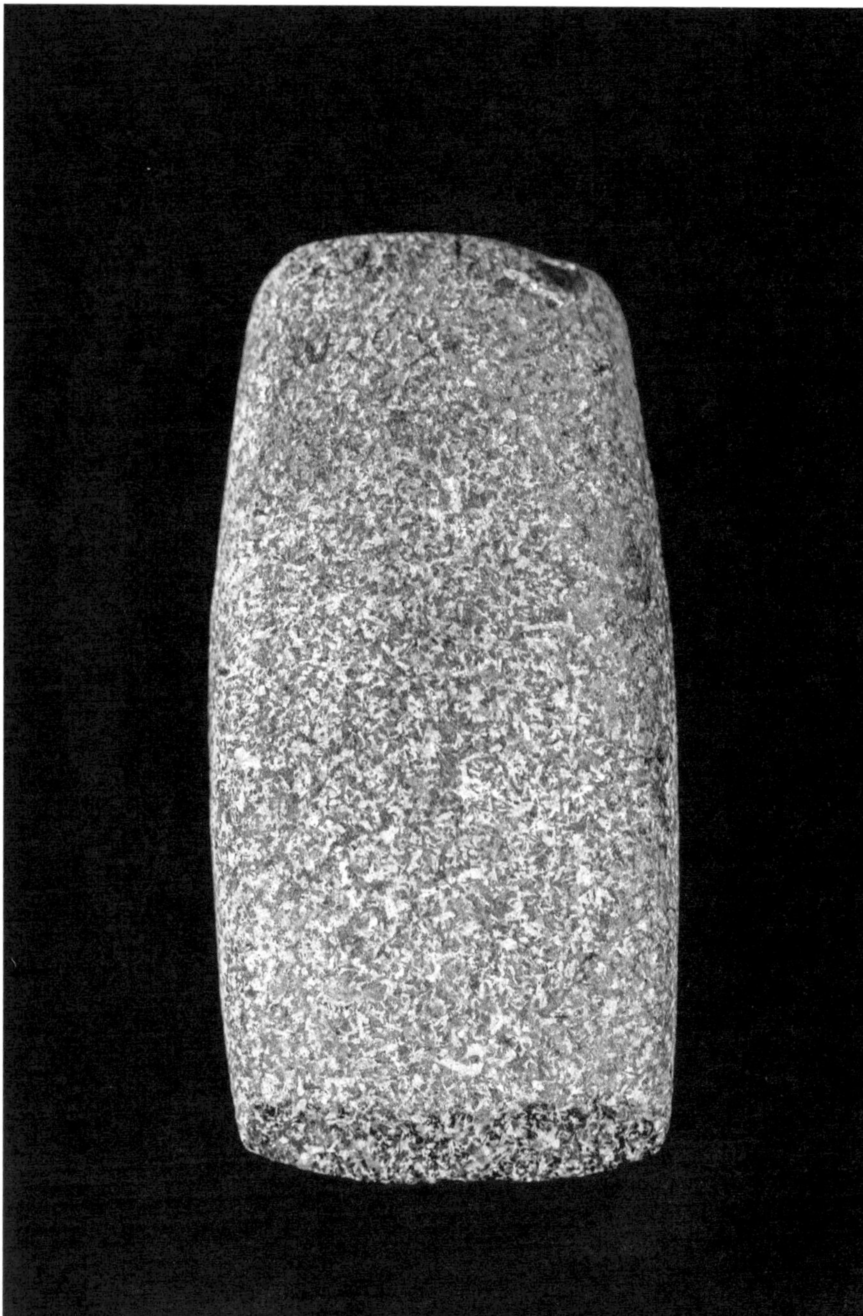

Late Woodland Period celt. *Courtesy of Steve Snodgress.*

the "Late Woodland sites are one of the more frequently identified sites within the region."[108]

It appears that "[a]t European contact, Indiana was apparently partially vacant of native people."[109] Perhaps archaeologists have yet to uncover the necessary artifacts from the area to form a better understanding, or the available evidence has not yet been properly synthesized. It is also possible that the Native Americans in Indiana at the time of European contact had dispersed due to disease, famine or warfare. Researchers, however, have concluded the following based on the available evidence:

> *In very general terms, the last 600 years prior to European expansion into Indiana can be described as a period during which prehistoric peoples: 1) completed a shift to a largely sedentary, agricultural way of life; 2) followed a nucleated pattern of settlement that centered around villages or towns; and 3) established some level of ranked socio-economic organization. There is evidence that the social landscape may have been increasingly unpredictable by AD 1400. The period is not only marked by the rise of maize agriculture, but by considerable cultural complexity, as well as by widespread population movement and dispersal and evidence of violent conflict.*[110]

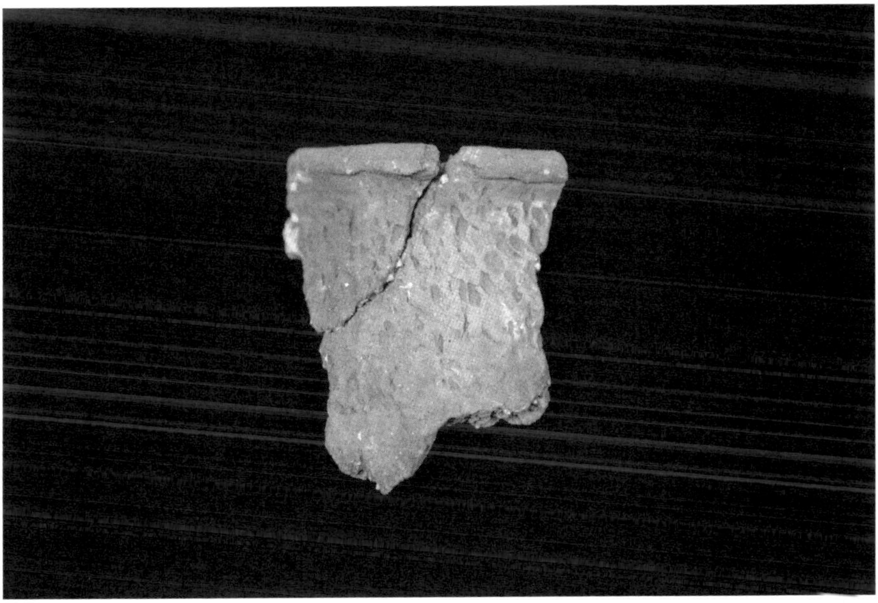

Castor pottery example. *Courtesy of Hamilton County Parks and Recreation.*

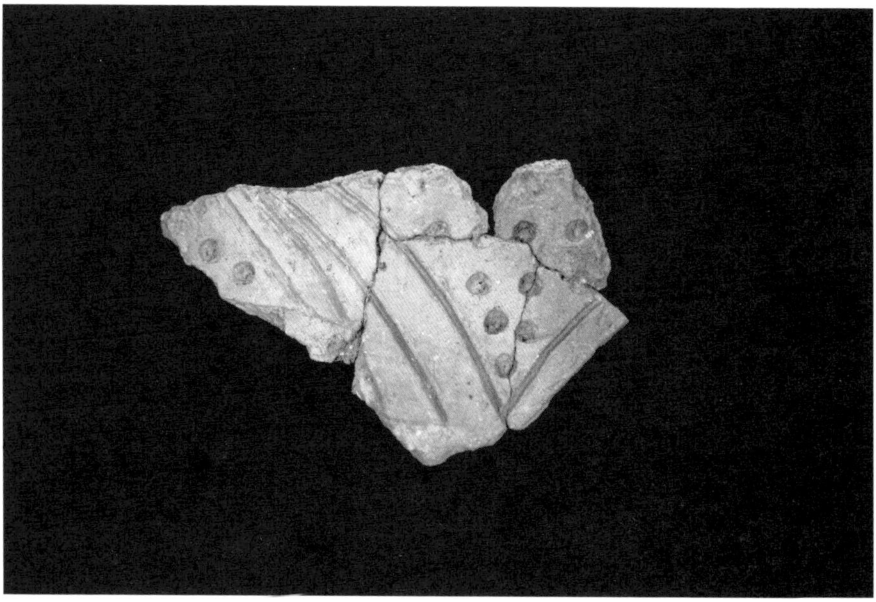

Oliver phase pottery in a Fort Ancient style. *Courtesy of Hamilton County Parks and Recreation.*

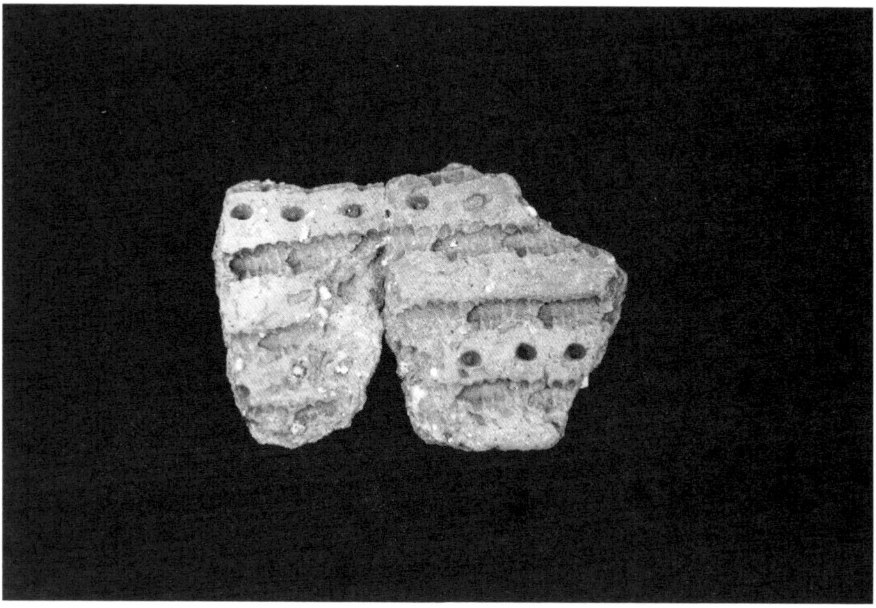

Western Basin pottery. *Courtesy of Hamilton County Parks and Recreation.*

Despite the limitations in our understanding, a few Late Pre-Contact period archaeological sites suggest that the area was inhabited by people whose remains are categorized as the Oneota Tradition, Oliver Phase, Castor Tradition and the Western Basin Tradition. The Oneota Tradition "occupation of Central Indiana is currently not well known."[111] Archaeological remains suggest that the Oneota Tradition was centered on what is now northern Illinois and Wisconsin from 900 CE until first contact with Europeans.[112] The Oliver Phase Culture is defined as a "mixing of Middle Fort Ancient and Great Lakes cultural elements to create a distinct group that occupied the White River drainage between about A.D. 1200 to 1450."[113]

Noted for their distinct ceramic styles, the Western Basin Tradition Culture is the "loosely defined designation for the Late Prehistoric farming populations ranged around the western edge of Lake Erie…who shared a number of characteristics, such as pottery decoration, burial practices, and a settlement pattern of scattered farmsteads and small hamlets."[114] Starting in the Middle Woodland Period, the Western Basin Tradition had four phases: Gibralter, 500–700 CE; Riviere au Vase, 700–1000 CE; Younge, 1000–1200 CE; and Springwells, 1200–1300 CE.[115] While evidence of the Western Basin Tradition exists in east-central Indiana, the Castor Phase appears as a well-documented cultural phase, existing in central Indiana roughly 1100–1500 CE.[116] The Castor Phase is generally defined as a cultural group in central Indiana that produced pottery consistent with the Western Basin Tradition, with "large sites and at least six different structure types, including large paired communal structures."[117] The most prominent archaeological site from this era is located at the Strawtown Koteewi Park in the modern village of Strawtown.

EAST-CENTRAL INDIANA IN THE MIDDLE: FORT ANCIENT AND MIDDLE MISSISSIPPIAN CULTURES

During this same time period, east-central Indiana was sandwiched between two other prominent earthwork-building cultures, the Middle Mississippian Culture, centered near present-day St. Louis Missouri, and the Fort Ancient Culture, in western and southern Ohio. It is likely that both cultures had an influence on the various Late Pre-Contact peoples in central Indiana. Flourishing approximately from 900 to 1750 CE, the Fort Ancient people "started to adopt a way of life that depended significantly on the production of domesticated plant foods. Although hunting, gathering, and collecting continued to be important, a large-scale dependence on maize, supplemented strongly by beans, along with squash, sunflowers, and chenopods, developed in the region for the first time."[118] Fort Ancient peoples also constructed earthworks and mounds, including palisade structures.

The Middle Mississippian Culture flourished near present-day St. Louis, with major activity starting approximately in 1050 CE. They also constructed large earthwork mounds, albeit for very different purposes than the mortuary and ceremonial structures built by earlier Adena and Hopewell peoples. Mississippian mounds were much larger than Early and Middle Woodland Period earthworks. Mounds of significance built by the Middle Mississippian Culture can be found at Cahokia near present-day St. Louis; Kincaid Mounds near present-day Paducah, Kentucky; at Angel Mounds near present-day Evansville, Indiana; and at several other sites located at or near the confluence of the Ohio and Mississippi Rivers. Evidence is sparse showing an interaction between Fort Ancient and Mississippian Cultures with the Late Pre-Contact period Oliver, Oneota, Western-Basin and Castor Cultures. However, some archaeological sites, such as the Bowen site in present-day Indianapolis, suggest some interaction between the surrounding

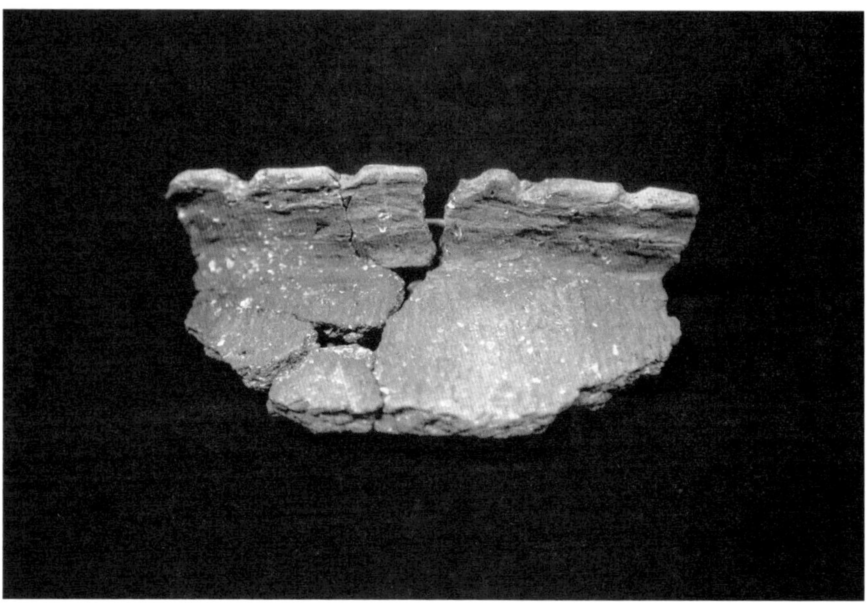

Oneota or Mississippian pottery. *Courtesy of Hamilton County Parks and Recreation.*

moundbuilding cultures and the Oliver Phase peoples.[119] Specifically, "the Oliver Phase, with its seeming combination of elements from many sources, reflects something of the cultural foment occurring during the early period of Mississippian development."[120]

The aggregate of our pre-contact Native American knowledge for east-central Indiana derives from an archaeological record that is incomplete and not entirely understood. We probably will never know the specific details of these cultures in the way we know and understand the post-contact Native Americans. We do know that the post-contact Native Americans living in Indiana—such as the Miami, Shawnee, Lenape and Potawatami "were late migrants into the area."[121] While these groups certainly had pre-contact ancestors, the possibility of connecting pre- and post-contact groups in Indiana is not realistic, or even likely. As James Kellar summarized, "In sum, to relate prehistory to history requires that American Indian ethnic groups be identified through unique house styles, pottery, tools, or other material objects accessible to archaeologists. However, in Indiana, no such body of data exists, or is likely to be recovered."[122] Therefore, the early Native American cultures in Indiana will likely remain forever shrouded in mystery.

Part II

East-Central Indiana After European Contact

Chapter 4

Native American Contact with Europeans in Indiana

The French were the first Europeans to step foot in what is now the state of Indiana in the 1670s.[123] Over time, French Canadians began to colonize the interior of North America along the Great Lakes and the Mississippi River. By the early 1700s, the French monarch Louis XIV had renewed European interest in the Mississippi watershed.[124] The entirety of the French interests in the New World became centered on Quebec in the north and Louisiana in the south, where "the dividing line [ran] east and west through central Indiana, near Terre Haute."[125] The Wabash River—known to the French as the Ouabache from the original Native name *Ouabouskigou*[126]—became an important French-controlled waterway, as it connected their two main North America interests. In the ensuing decades, the French built blockhouses, forts and trading posts along the Wabash River at present-day Fort Wayne, known to the French as Fort Miami near the Miami Native American village Kekionga; Ouiatenon near present-day Lafayette near a Wea village site of the same name; and at Fort Vincennes near present-day Vincennes, near the Piankashaw village Chipkawke.[127]

Fort Ouiatenon was taken from the French by a coalition of Algonquian-speaking Native Americans during Pontiac's Rebellion. From that point, the fort passed back to the French and then on to the Americans. Ultimately, Ouiatenon was destroyed on the orders of George Washington during the Northwest Indian War. Fort Miami shared a similar fate, passing back and forth between French, Native and British powers. American forces under General "Mad" Anthony Wayne took control of Fort Miami and renamed

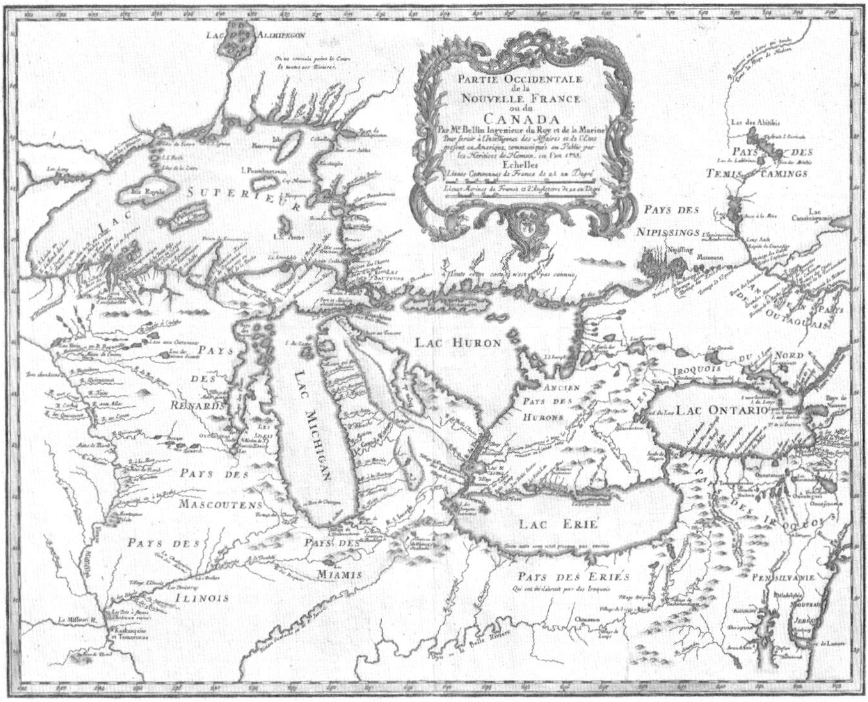

1755 map of New France by Jacques Nicholas Bellin. *Courtesy of Wikicommons.*

it Fort Wayne. Fort Vincennes fared a little better, having been taken over by Chickasaw Native Americans in 1735; the French ultimately surrendered the fort to the British in the French and Indian War, whereupon it was renamed Fort Sackville and was nominally defended. During the American Revolution, George Rogers Clark captured the fort during the Siege of Vincennes and held it for the new American government, renaming it Fort Patrick Henry. The Americans built two different forts near Fort Patrick Henry and named them Knox. The nearby city of Vincennes remained a trading post of French families, thriving after the conclusion of the Northwest Indian War, and having served as the Indiana Territory capital until 1813.[128]

The French impact on the indigenous tribes living in the area at the time cannot be understated. Each successive wave of Euro-American powers possessed different protocols governing their relationships with the indigenous groups. The French generally saw their interactions with indigenous cultures based on mutually beneficial trade, with fur being the primary component of all economic transactions. The French and Native societies saw reciprocal advantages in the fur trade, but never fully integrated. The interplay between the French, British and American societies with the indigenous tribes in Indiana is complex, constantly changing, and never consistent. Early frontier Indiana life was occasionally violent between Euro-American settlers and Native Americans; however, "much of the relationship between Native Americans and Europeans was mundane, the routine of unexceptional events that makes up the bulk of human history—trading, talking, eating, sleeping with each other, bearing and raising children."[129] The latter two seemed especially unique to French and Native interaction in Indiana, where "there was significant miscegenation, almost always between French men and Indian women. The relative scarcity of European women made casual sexual relationships almost inevitable. But often they were relatively permanent. Several families in late eighteenth-century Vincennes claimed descent from both European and Indian ancestors."[130] French traders continually show up in the annals of Lenape history during their time in east-central Indiana, and prominent French-Miami family names such as Richardville, Hackley and Godfroy appear again and again throughout the eighteenth- and nineteenth century histories of Indiana.

The Post-Contact Tribes of Indiana

The Native American tribes documented after the first European contact in what is now Indiana were migrants from other areas. As European colonizers entered North America, the indigenous political dynamics drastically changed. War, disease, fur trading and European meddling contributed to massive indigenous population movements, war and death. The Miami were one of the first groups to move into what is now Indiana because of this new imbalance. The powerful Iroquois tribes around the eastern Great Lakes began pushing into western areas during a series of conflicts known as the Beaver Wars. Armed with European guns, the Iroquois pushed the Miami and others south. The Miami, an Algonquian-speaking ethnic group once centered in present-day Wisconsin, moved south in the 1640s, establishing village sites across northern and central Indiana, with primary residences along the upper Wabash River and the Mississinewa River.[131] Along with many other indigenous tribes, the Miami probably suffered heavily from European diseases that spread throughout North America along their trade routes, long before their first contact with Europeans.[132] By the time the French began documenting the Miami in Indiana, their culture had already radically changed.

The Miami are easily the most powerful and well-known indigenous group in Indiana during the early Euro-American period. Known variously as Oumamink, Maumee or Memilounique by the French; Tuwéhtuwe by the Lenape; and Twightwees by many early Americans, the Miami played a powerful position during Indiana's territorial development, the Northwest Indian War and the War of 1812.

Like the Miami, the Potawatomi were pushed south from the Western Great Lakes area during the Beaver Wars. Both groups were generally very open, allowing neighboring tribes to settle on their land: "Branches of the Pottawattamie, [Shawnee], Delaware, and Kickapoo tribes, were, at different periods of time, permitted to enter, and reside at various places, within the boundaries of the large territory which was claimed by the Miamis."[133] The Potawatomi referred to themselves as Neshnabé, whereas Potawatomi was the exonym given to them by the Ojibwe. The Potawatomi lived in several villages in northern Indiana including Macon, Menominee, Menoquet, Tippecanoe and Winamac.

The Kickapoo, another Algonquian-speaking people, had settlements near present-day Terre Haute as the French first found them. The Kickapoo originated in northern Ohio and southern Michigan but were displaced to present-day Wisconsin by the Iroquois. A band of Kickapoo moved into what is now Indiana, forming the Wabash Confederation with other indigenous groups in the area, including the Wea, Mascouten and the Piankashaw. The Indiana Kickapoo were known as the Vermilion Tribe or Vermilion Band of Kickapoo. The Mascouten shared similar circumstances, having moved from southern Michigan to Wisconsin, ultimately residing in the southern Wabash River Valley.

This same area of land along the Wabash, from approximately present-day Lafayette to Vincennes, was home to two strongly affiliated Miami bands or subtribes: the Wea and the Piankashaw.[134] Both groups became the primary parties of the Wabash Confederation. The Wea—concentrated at the Wea Plains near Ouiatenon, Lafayette and Terre Haute—spoke an Algonquian Miami dialect and were also pushed into the Wabash River area from Wisconsin after the Beaver Wars. During their time in the Indiana territory, the French referred to them as Ouiatenons. Toward the south, past the Mascouten and Kickapoo villages, the Piankashaw had several village sites around present-day Vincennes. The Piankashaw and Wea are best understood as subtribes of the Miami, or strongly affiliated bands that shared a similar language, culture and way of life. The Wea and Piankashaw were part of "six Miami-speaking groups. Three of the groups, namely the Wea,

Piankashaw and Atchatchakangouen, later became tribes. The other three groups, the Kilatika, Pepicokia and Mengakonkia, gradually joined other Miami groups and disappeared from the historic record by the eighteenth century."[135] Disease, warfare and displacement rendered the Miami relationship with the affiliated bands in Indiana complex. Throughout this period of territorial history, the early Indiana historians, missionaries and settlers also identify smaller indigenous populations of Wyandot, Cherokee, Ojibwe and various Illiniwek groups.

Two other prominent Native American nations lived in what is now Indiana throughout the early territorial period: the Shawnee and the Lenape. The Lenape's history in Indiana is the primary focus of the ensuing chapters, but it is critical to mention at this point that the Lenape were invited by the Miami to live along the west fork of the White River at the conclusion of the Northwest Indian War. Although there were probably Lenape villages in Indiana as early as the 1760s, the main body lived along the west fork of the White River from the 1790s until 1821.

The Shawnee had village sites in southeastern Indiana and western Ohio in the later 1700s, but their early history "is shrouded in uncertainty."[136] Scholars and "ethnographers disagree over what areas the tribe occupied before the mid-seventeenth century, but by the 1650s they were living in southern Ohio and northern Kentucky."[137] By the 1700s, bands of Shawnee were living across what is now the eastern United States along the Gulf Coast, the Delaware River Valley, present-day Georgia, Illinois, Alabama, Maryland and Pennsylvania.[138] By the mid-1700s, the Shawnee had coalesced around the Scioto River Valley, which "also marked the last time that such tribal cohesion would occur. By 1750, the Shawnees were divided into five semiautonomous political units or bands."[139]

Beaver Wars

The Beaver Wars were a series of violent conflicts in the Great Lakes area in the mid-1600s between French-supported Algonquian-speaking indigenous tribes against Iroquois groups backed by the British and the Dutch. The result of these clashes fundamentally altered indigenous life, alliances and territorial arrangements around the Great Lakes and eastern North America. Speaking a different set of languages than their Algonquian neighbors, the Iroquois dominated the Great Lakes area politically through trade and warfare, while maintaining a centralized military strategy with European weapons.

The term "Iroquois" reflects different indigenous groups that spoke similar languages with shared customs. In regard to the Beaver Wars, historians agree that the Iroquois bands aligned together, initially consisting of five tribes, referred to as the Iroquois Confederacy, or the Five Nations. The original five tribes included the Mohawk, the Onondaga, the Oneida, the Cayuga and the Seneca. Later, the Tuscarora became part of the confederacy after they moved from present-day North Carolina, rendering the confederacy the Six Nations.[140] The Mohawk tended to politically dominate the Iroquois Confederacy throughout the Beaver Wars. Iroquois was an exonym given to the groups by the French. The preferred indigenous autonym is Haudenosaunee.

The Iroquois became reliant on the fur trade after early European contact. Overhunting gradually depopulated fur-bearing animals in the eastern forests. The Iroquois, having adopted fur hunting as a primary way of life, became entirely reliant on European trade. To sustain this, efforts turned toward war as a means to secure a dominant position in fur acquisition. As the Iroquois saw it, they had little choice. To stay in existence, they "had either to find new hunting grounds or to capture a position as middlemen."[141] Pushing west and southeast from their ancestral homelands on the southern shores of Lake Ontario and armed with European guns, the powerful Iroquois Confederacy overpowered, defeated, absorbed or otherwise dominated their Algonquian-speaking neighbors, pushing many, as we have seen, out of their ancestral homes and into southern lands. Throughout the middle decades of the 1600s, the Iroquois pushed farther south into the Alleghenies and west into present-day Indiana. Tragically, "As commercial ventures, however, the Beaver Wars as a whole were a failure."[142] During this time, it should be noted that some historians find the Lenape politically subservient to the Iroquois Confederacy.[143] Controlling the "French" land between the Great Lakes and the Ohio River, west of the Appalachian Mountains, the Iroquois allowed other Native American nations displaced by Europeans along the Atlantic seaboard to settle in the interior.[144] By the end of the 1600s, the Iroquois had made peace with the French at the Great Peace of Montreal in 1701, which ceased hostilities between the French, their Algonquian-speaking allies and the Iroquois. Many of the displaced tribes moved back to their ancestral homelands or to new locations. At this time, the Miami and their affiliated tribes moved into northern Indiana and the Shawnee returned to southern Ohio. The Beaver War hostilities ceased in the early 1700s.

THE FRENCH AND INDIAN WAR

Frontier violence cannot be understated during the 1600s and the 1700s in the northern Appalachian Mountain area. While isolated incidents of violence existed throughout the period, the Beaver Wars, the French and Indian War, Pontiac's Rebellion, the American Revolution, the Northwest Indian War and the War of 1812 consisted of extremely violent incidents between and among Native Americans and Europeans. The French and Indian War was particularly brutal in the Ohio country. Fought between 1754 and 1763, the conflict saw British America allied with the Iroquois-speaking tribes against New France and their many Algonquian-speaking confederates, including the Lenape, the Shawnee, Ojibwe and Potawatomi. The war between the two great colonial powers was fought "for the possession of the Ohio Valley"[145] and was "essentially a commercial struggle for the fur trade."[146] The French ultimately were defeated in the conflict, having ceded much of their territory to Great Britain at the Treaty of Paris in 1763. While pockets of French traders stayed in what is now Indiana, most of the French moved north to Quebec or down to New Orleans. As the French left, so did their relatively fair policies toward Native Americans in the Ohio, Michigan, Indiana and Illinois areas. As the British assumed control of these lands, their policies toward indigenous groups were significantly more oppressive. The Indiana historian Logan Esarey defined this relationship bluntly:

> *The English soldiers, and especially the English traders, were extremely offensive to the Indians. The soldiers refused to mingle with the Indians, refused to sell them guns and ammunition, and refused to allow them to loaf inside the forts. The English fur traders, taken by and large, were the worst class of men in America. They had the characteristic commercial disregard of sentiment. To them the Indian was a very inferior being, to be cheated, outraged, robbed or murdered as best suited their money-making purposes. The traders had no regard for the helpless settlers on the frontier so long as they themselves escaped with plunder and life.*[147]

PONTIAC'S REBELLION

The British attitude under General Jeffrey Amherst was especially cruel toward Native Americans, including passing out blankets infected with smallpox.[118] He even "ordered western commanders to limit the gifts they gave to the Indians, as well as ammunition, and to stop the sale of rum and other liquor. From Amherst's perspective, these sensible moves designed to encourage economy and restrain the Indians. But they were little short of disastrous in Indiana, where the exchange of gifts and goods had been at the heart of [French] relationships for decades." British settlers also began pouring across the Appalachian Mountains, disrupting the already tenuous territorial holds of the indigenous populations. As a result, several Native bands formed a loose confederation influenced and partially led by the Ottawa chief Pontiac and the Seneca chief Guyasuta.

This confederation of Algonquian-speaking groups and Iroquois bands allied together to drive out the British. The major tribal combatants included warriors from bands of Wyandot, Kickapoo, Lenape, Mascouten, Miami, Mingo, Ottawa, Ojibwe, Piankeshaw, Potawatomi, Seneca, Shawnee and Wea. The confederation marked the first time a diverse array of Algonquian-speaking bands allied together to drive out European colonizers west of the Appalachians. Similar alliances would be forged again during the Northwest Indian War and Tecumseh's Rebellion.

The conflict began when Pontiac attacked and sieged Fort Detroit in 1763. Inspired by his efforts, smaller forts throughout the area were attacked and destroyed, including Fort Miami at present-day Fort Wayne and Fort Ouiatenon near present-day Lafayette. Fort Miami was taken when the Native American mistress of the British commander, Ensign Robert Holmes, "convinced him to leave the fort, whereupon he was captured. The small garrison then quickly surrendered."[119] Pontiac lifted the siege at Fort Detroit and spent much of the remainder of the conflict in the Wabash River Valley area. The British dispatched George Croghan in 1765 to sue for peace with Pontiac. Croghan was captured by Mascouten and Kickapoo warriors along the Wabash and taken to Native-controlled Fort Ouiatenon. Croghan was treated fairly and secured reconciliation agreements with Pontiac and four different Native American nations.[150] The British gained the upper hand with a series of military expeditions and individual treaties. Ultimately, Pontiac's Rebellion slightly improved the British policies toward Native Americans under the Royal Proclamation of 1763, which legally honored indigenous sovereignty west of the Appalachian Mountains, at least on paper.

The American Revolutionary War

As was the case in the French and Indian War, indigenous bands west of the Appalachians were divided in their loyalties, with some siding with the new American government while others backed the British. Many attempted neutrality. Even among the various Native bands, it was not uncommon to see warriors from the same "tribe" fighting on both sides. The concept of a "tribe" as a centralized political group did not exist universally at this time, and therefore, centralized political authority was generally uncommon in most groups. While some indigenous groups were more politically organized, it is best to think of the various Native Americans as different ethnic groups, with shared cultural, linguistic and religious characteristics. The complexity of the American Revolutionary War alliances mirrors the complexity of philosophical beliefs, individual interests and pragmatic points of view held by each Native group during the war.

Many Iroquois fought alongside the British during the American Revolution, although some Mohawk and Oneida fought with the Americans. Many indigenous groups saw a unified coalition of colonies as a threat to their own territorial claims. The main body of the Lenape attempted to stay neutral, although some warriors fought with the British. Many Shawnee fought with the British, seeing them as the lesser of two evils. Very little American Revolutionary War action took place in what is now Indiana. The Wabash River Valley was controlled by the British, though minimally defended. The Miami, therefore, largely stayed out of the war but were "nominally pro-British"[151] and traded with French and Spanish groups along the Mississippi River.[152] Some of the tribes in the Ohio country, including the Miami, were tasked to "watch the Ohio River especially and destroy all Americans attempting to pass."[153] In 1780, a French colonel named Augustin La Balme led a force of Canadian Frenchmen from Vincennes and attacked and destroyed the Miami village Kekionga near present-day Fort Wayne. La Balme intended to move north with his force and capture Detroit from the British but was attacked by Miami chief Little Turtle, who killed La Balme and his men.[154]

La Balme's ill-fated attempt to take Detroit was likely inspired by General George Rogers Clark's taking of Fort Sackville at Vincennes in 1779. After taking British forts in the Illinois country, Clark took control of Fort Sackville without firing a shot. Clark retook Sackville in late February, having lost the fort to the British commander Henry Hamilton. Clark went on to sack several British-backed Shawnee villages in the Ohio country with a militia of Virginians and Kentuckians in 1780.

The hostilities ended in 1783 with the signing of the Treaty of Paris, where the British ceded to the Americans all land south of Detroit, west of the Appalachians and west to the Mississippi river. They did so without conferring with their indigenous allies. The Iroquois Confederacy had lost much of its potency at the conclusion of the war, and the Old Northwest Territory, having passed to the new American government, became lawless.[155] This new dynamic set the stage for the second great Algonquian confederacy against Euro-American colonization.

THE NORTHWEST INDIAN WAR

The second major Algonquian Native American confederation involved a series of conflicts known as the Northwest Indian War and lasted from 1785 to 1795. Following the American Revolution, the territory obtained from the British—which consisted of the present-day states Ohio, Indiana, Illinois, Michigan, Wisconsin and part of Minnesota—was organized as the Northwest Territory. The new American government sought to sell these lands to Euro-American settlers in order to pay off war debts, despite the territory being controlled by various indigenous tribes. In response to American pressure, several Native American groups formed the Western Confederacy, a loose organization of the Great Lakes area Native American tribes, to fight American settlement. As with Pontiac's Rebellion, not every indigenous band in the area took part, but many did, including warriors from bands of Miami, Wyandot, Lenape, Kickapoo, the Wabash Confederation, Potawatomi, Ojibwe, Odawa, Kaskaskia and Lower Cherokee. In 1785, warriors in the Western Confederacy began raiding settler villages in the Ohio country. United States generals Benjamin Logan and George Rogers Clark each led a small group of Kentucky militiamen to raid Shawnee and Miami villages, respectively. While Logan gained military advantage in burning several Shawnee villages, Clark did not.[156]

The United States government ordered General Josiah Harmar to invade and attack Shawnee and Miami villages from the Ohio River in 1790. Traveling up the Wabash, Harmar sent Colonel John Hardin to attack the Miami village of Kekionga near modern-day Fort Wayne. More than one thousand Miami warriors, led by Chief Little Turtle, defeated Hardin.[157] A series of other conflicts in central Indiana and Ohio resulted with the Americans reeling from several failed attempts to subdue the Western

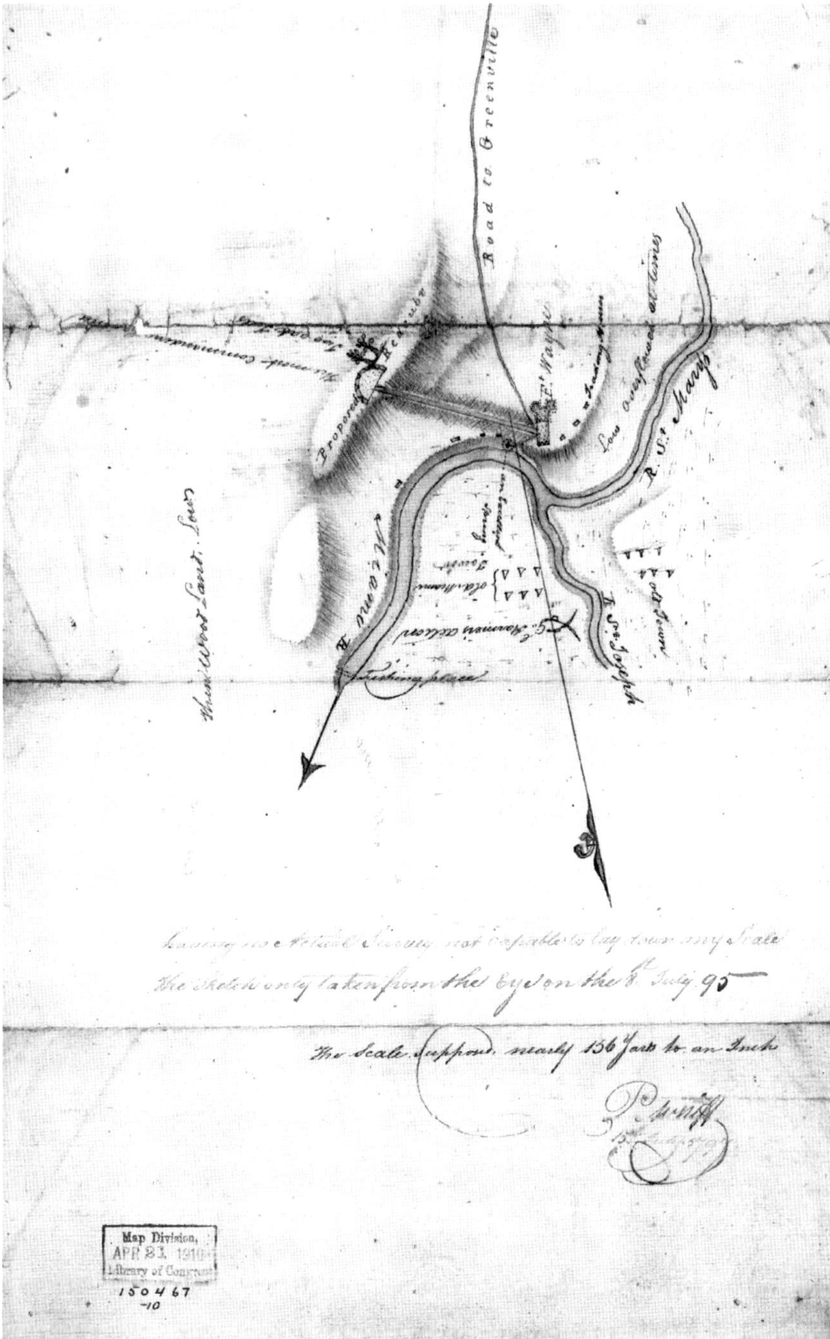

1795 map of Kekionga (Fort Wayne). *Courtesy of the Library of Congress.*

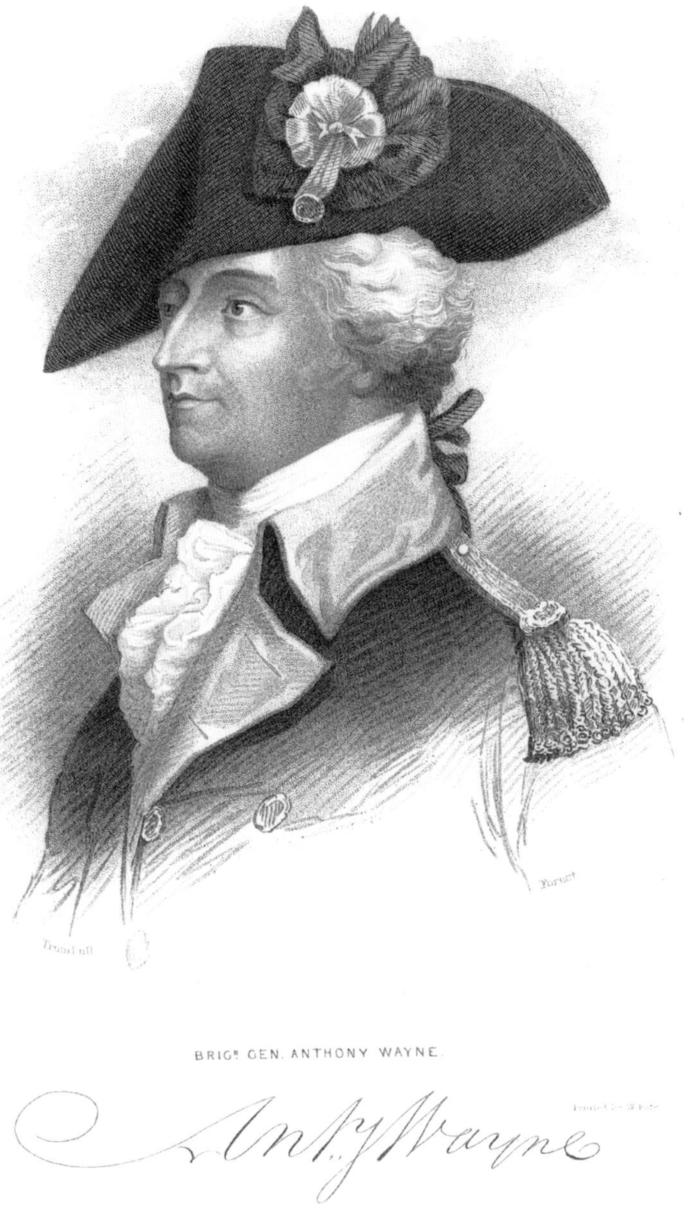

American General "Mad" Anthony Wayne by John Trumbull. Wayne defeated the Western Confederacy at the Battle of Fallen Timbers in 1794. *Courtesy of the Library of Congress.*

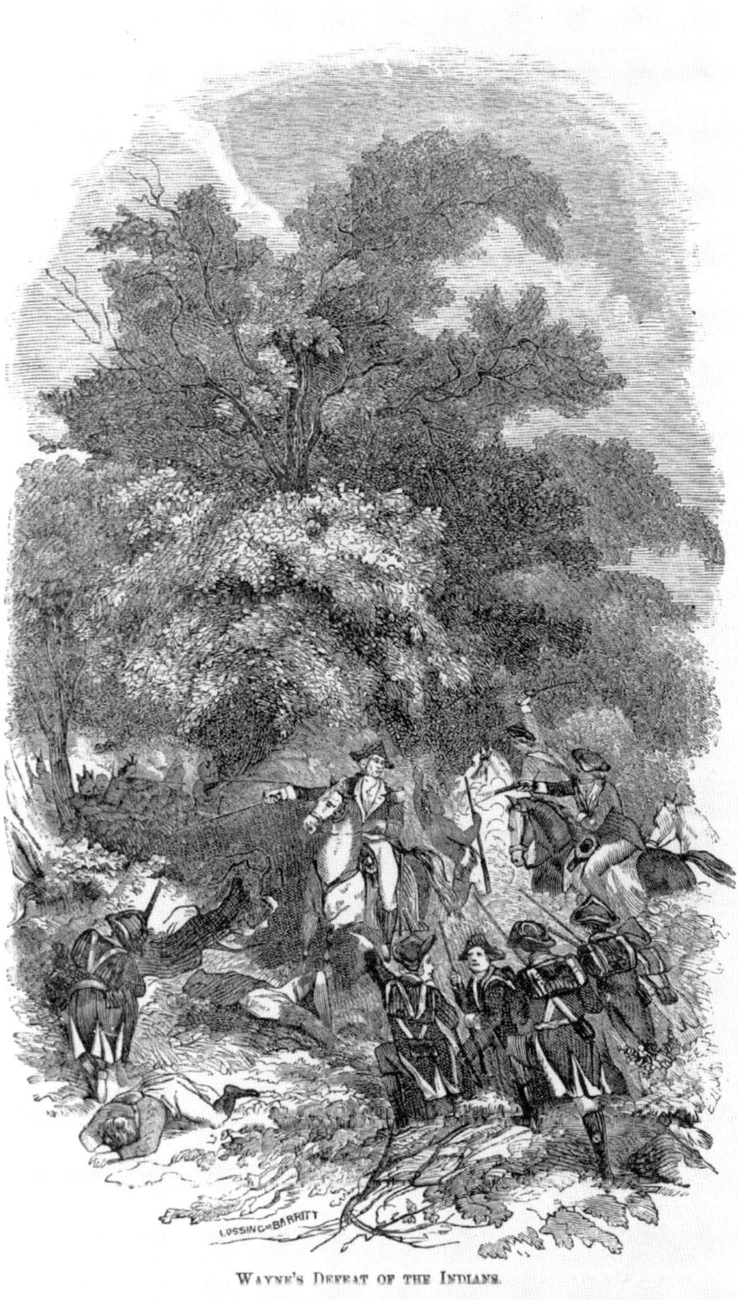

Battle of Fallen Timbers. *Courtesy of the Library of Congress.*

Confederacy. Supported by the British from the north, the Western Confederacy consistently held its ground; so much so that the American major Francis Hamtramck concluded that "the Americans would never be able to end the war as long as the British held the northern posts."[158]

President George Washington ordered the Northwest Territory's governor, Arthur St. Clair, to destroy the Miami along the Wabash. Leading a force of about 1,000 men, St. Clair met Western Confederacy warriors near present-day Fort Recovery, Ohio, on November 4, 1791. Led by Miami chief Little Turtle, Shawnee chief Blue Jacket and Lenape chief Buckhongehelas, St. Clair's army was crushed in what came to be known as the "Battle of the Wabash" or "St. Claire's Defeat." This event resulted in 933 casualties, more than 630 of which were deaths. Numerous captured American militiamen were executed in the ensuing days. A furious Washington then ordered a well-trained army under General "Mad" Anthony Wayne to accomplish what the other territorial generals could not. Marching north from Cincinnati, Wayne's force met and defeated the Western Confederacy on August 20, 1794, at the Battle of Fallen Timbers near present-day Toledo, Ohio. At the conclusion of the battle, Wayne marched south to Kekionga and built "Fort Wayne."[159]

The following year, on August 3, leaders from the Western Confederacy met with Wayne at Greenville, Ohio, to sign the Treaty of Greenville. This treaty essentially waived all indigenous land claims in present-day Ohio. At this point in time, the Lenape and Shawnee were spread across the Ohio country, with the former having no lands, village sites or legal territory. Little Turtle pledged full allegiance to the United States, having "resigned himself to the inevitability of the Americans"[160] and moved with many of his people near Fort Wayne. In the year 1803, Ohio became the seventeenth state, with part of the remaining Northwest Territory eventually organized as the Indiana Territory. William Henry Harrison became the first Indiana territorial governor.

Chapter 5

The Lenape

The Lenape were an Algonquian people living in the Hudson and Delaware River Valleys at the time of first European contact in the 1520s. They lived in all or part of the present-day states of New York, New Jersey, Delaware and Pennsylvania. The Lenape at this time are best understood as an ethnic group who lived in a series of culturally related villages,[161] spoke related Algonquian dialects, or languages,[162] and "were drawn from a large number of small, dispersed and relatively autonomous groups."[163] A centralized political structure with a titular chief did not exist at the time of European contact. The Lenape were simply "politically unorganized."[164] The autonomous Lenape villages had *sakimas*, or "village wise men," in charge "who served the chieftains in the role of councilors, and participated in the decision making."[165]

At the time of first European contact, the Lenape generally lived in villages falling into "three principal dispersed and autonomous geographic"[166] and linguistic groups, which included the Munsees in the north, the Northern Unamis along the river valleys to the south and the Southern Unami farther south in the Schuylkill River valley and around what is now Delaware Bay. These three Lenape linguistic/geographic areas consisted of many different bands of villages, including Navisink, Raritan, Hackinsack, Aquackanonk, Haverstraw, Minisink, Waoraneck, Warranawonkong and Katskill—about forty in all.[167] Early European settlers would often name the Lenape bands after the specific stream they lived near. "For instance the natives living on Sickoneysinck Creek…were called Sickoneysinck Indians…those living on the Rancocas Creek were called Rancocas Indians; those living on the Brandywine, were known as Brandywine Indians."[168]

The *Lenape* autonym means "the people." The term *Delaware*, used consistently after the year 1700, derived from Lord Thomas West de la Warr, the second governor of Virginia Colony. The indigenous groups in the area were known as De la Warr's Indians and later just Delaware Indians.[169] Trowbridge also wrote that the Lenape were sometimes referred as the Oaponohkee[170] by other tribes. Oaponohkee "is derived from Oápun—Day, Daylight, and means the men from the East, or where the day comes."[171] *Lenape* is inexact when describing all the peoples in this area and is imprecise when used to collectively define all the groups in this region, at this particular time. Regardless of which term historians use to describe them, the term *Lenape* at the time of first contact describes different, independent village communities with a shared culture and related languages.[172] The Lenape had Iroquois to their west, Mahican to their north, Wappinger and Pequot speakers to the east on present-day Long Island and Connecticut and Nanticoke and Piscataway speakers to the south.

The Lenape living in northern villages below the Mahican came to be known as Munsee after the principal village Minisink. They spoke a different, albeit related, Lenape language than their southern neighbors.[173] The Munsee "have also been variously referred to as the Minsis, Monseys, Munsis, Montheys, and Minisinks."[174] Often one village would politically control adjacent villages, or "the people living in villages along the same stream

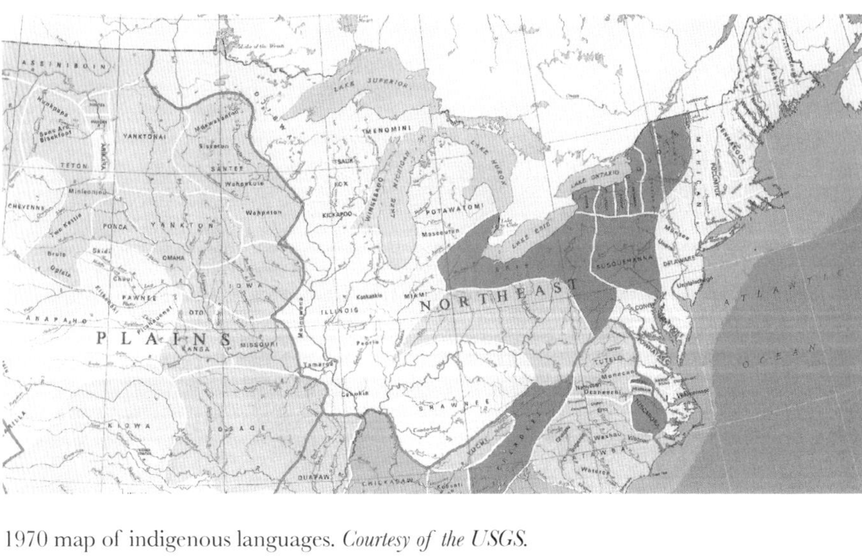

1970 map of indigenous languages. *Courtesy of the USGS.*

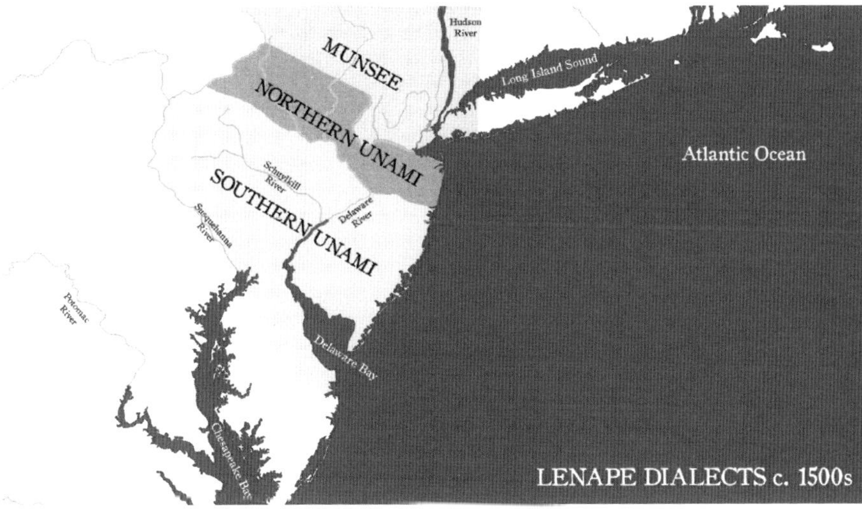

Lenape dialect map, circa 1500s. *Author's collection.*

constituted what can best be described as a band, and the most influential village chief may have functioned as the nominal head of the band."[175] The Minisink were probably the foremost Munsee-speaking village[176] and as the Lenape bands were pushed inland, the Minisink probably politically controlled the other northern bands that in time became Munsee. *Munsee* in the Lenape language meant "from the stony country/rocky area." Over the centuries, the Munsee were sometimes considered by their Unami brethren as a separate tribe, or perhaps a sub-tribe given that they differed in "dialect and other physical and cultural characteristics,"[177] but are considered by many historians, linguists and anthropologists as Lenape.

To the south of the Munsee lived the many Unami-speaking Lenape. Unami, which means "the downriver people closest to the ocean,"[178] spoke a different Lenape dialect than the Munsee. Over the centuries, Unami speakers constituted the largest part or main body of the nation as they were pushed farther inland to east-central Indiana. Linguists divide Unami speakers into Northern and Southern categories. A southern group of villages, referred to as the Unalachtigo, or "those that live next to the ocean," was at one time considered a distinct geographic/linguistic group.[179] There is some dispute about the Unalachtigo, as they were probably just a southern Unami-speaking village that merged with the other southern Unami very early on,[180] or they may have been or were affiliated with the Nanticoke.[181] Regardless, the terms *Munsee* and *Unami* were essentially "geographic terms"[182] referring to the general region of Lenape villages that spoke similar dialects. It is best to think of Munsee and Unami as linguistic classifications based on the geographic locations of those who spoke the dialect. They do not reflect political organization or significant cultural variation for those living in the Delaware and Hudson River Valleys when Europeans first came to North America. Over time, "As the remnant bands left their homeland and settled in new locations, the terms *Unami* and *Munsee* clung to them [and] came to be used in a political sense."[183]

All of the Lenape villages organized into three different matrilineal phratries, each of "which were further subdivided into ten to twelve clans"[184] at least by the middle 1700s. The matrilineal phratry system meant that children were born into the mother's family and that ancestry passed through female lineage. The three phratries were and still are the Wolf (or Tookseat), the Turtle (or Pokekooungo) and the Turkey (or Pullaook).[185] It is not uncommon in the literature to see the three phratries confused with the geographic/linguistic names Munsee, Northern Unami and Southern Unami. However, research has shown that "phratry members were located among all three of the divisions"[186] and were separate systems. So, for example, a Munsee speaker could be from the Wolf, Turtle or Turkey phratry, and an Unami speaker could also be from any one of the phratries. It is unknown whether the Lenape developed this system post-European contact as they moved inland or whether it was a system in place prior to colonization.[187] Shutt suggested that the "phratries appear to have served both as markers of difference but also as a way to expand the divide between Munsees and Unamis as these peoples came together"[188] in the interior. Regardless of the origins, this system was solidly in place by the time the Lenape arrived on the White River in Indiana.

Frederick Hodge[189] listed the phratry clans as:

> *Tookseat/Wolf Phratry: Maangreet (big feet), Weesoketko (yellow tree), Pasakunamon (pulling corn), Weyarnihkato (cave enterer), Tooshwarkama (across the river); Olumane (vermillion), Punaryou (dog standing by fireside), Kwineekcha (long body), Moonhartarne (digging), Nonharmin (pulling up stream), Longushharkarto (brush log), and Mawsootoh (bringing along).*
>
> *Pokekooungo/Turtle Phratry: Okahoki (ruler), Takoongoto (high bank shore), Seeharongoto (drawing down hill), Oleharkarmekarto (elector), Maharolukti (brave), Tungulugsi (smallest turtle), Welunungsi (little*

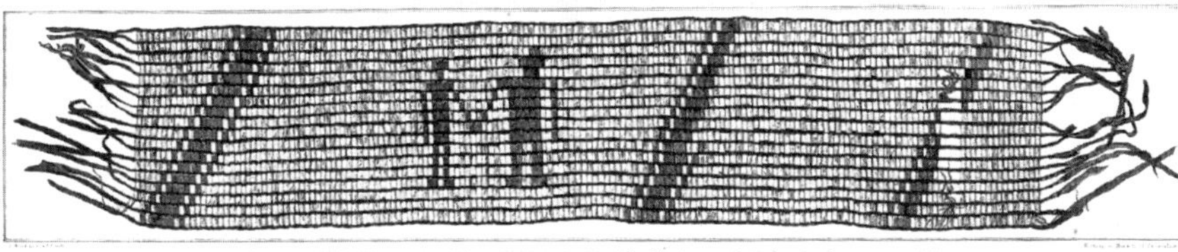

Wampum belt given to William Penn. *Courtesy of the Library of Congress.*

> *turtle), Leekwinai (snapping turtle), and Kwisaesekeetso (deer). Two other clans existed, but were lost as the Lenape moved further inland.*
>
> *Pullaook/Turkey Phratry: Moharala (big bird), Lelewayou (bird's cry), Mookwungwahoki (eye pain), Mooharmowikarnu (scratch the path), Opinghoki (opposum ground), Muhhowekaken (old shin), Tongonaoto (drift log), Noolamarlarmo (living in water), Muhkrentharne (root digger), Muhkarmhukse (red face), Koowahoke (pine region), and Oochuckhain (ground scratcher).*

At the first European contact, the Lenape hunted, fished, gathered and farmed small crops like squash and corn.[190] They lived in bark wigwams and wore clothing "made of animal skins, feathers, and plant fibers."[191] Like many of their Algonquian-speaking neighbors, the Lenape used elaborate strings of shell beads, known as wampum, as a form of ritual exchange; symbolic gestures for war, peace and agreements; storytelling; and as currency after European contact. Throughout the entire region, the Lenape were revered as the grandfather tribe by their neighbors. As such, they were "admitted priority of political rank and of their occupancy of the central home territory from which most of the cognate tribes had diverged."[192] The sakimas "did not have servants, possessed no more [wealth] than their native associates, and exercised very limited authority."[193] A chief's role in Lenape society "entailed both executive and ceremonial responsibilities, a strong democratic spirit governed and that of their people in what was an economic as well as political democracy."[194]

We may never know all the pre-contact Lenape cultural elements, as their way of life fundamentally changed following contact with Europeans. Disease, warfare, intermarriage and changing political alliances not only forced the Lenape farther inland, but also radically reoriented their social and political lives, along with their population. No one really knows for sure, but from the time of first European contact in the 1520s until the early 1800s, the Lenape population dropped precipitously from twenty thousand to two thousand individuals.[195] It is difficult to know how exactly the phratry/clan system existed prior to European contact; however, as the "independent Munsee and Unami bands coalesced in frontier villages, the political life of such groups followed a pattern by which the independent village sachems centralized under a clan-based governing body. The Delaware political system that emerged in the mid-eighteenth century consisted of three clan chiefs who represented three matrilineal clans, the Wolf, Turkey, and Turtle [where one] clan chief acted as the first among equals."[196] By the time the main body of Lenape lived in Indiana, they had politically organized with six titular chiefs, "three of whom are war and the others Council Chiefs."[197] The chiefs were elected by a council of wise men known as Lupwaaeenóáuk.[198] This Great Delaware Council "composed of chiefs and captains-as well as warriors and patriarchs-representing the three divisions."[199] The chiefs by this time were heavily involved in internal village life, while "affairs of consequence are never acted upon without the concurrence of the Lupwaaeenóáuk."[200] This council was consulted by chiefs for "all treaties, declarations of war"[201] and when those outside the Lenape wanted an "expression of their opinion as a body."[202]

Chapter 6

The Atlantic Coast to East-Central Indiana

The Lenape's migration from the Atlantic seaboard to east-central Indiana took place over about two hundred years. The move west was rife with tragedy and violence. As the Lenape were politically decentralized, the journey was also unorganized. This resulted in bands being scattered across what is now the eastern United States, north of the Ohio River and into present-day Canada. This history alone would take many volumes. For the sake of clarity, it is necessary to cover briefly the period for the necessary context of the White River Lenape. It is impossible to fully understand the Indiana period from the 1790s until 1821 without first comprehending the preceding circumstances.

European Contact

The Lenape made first contact with Europeans when Dutch traders began exchanging their goods for fur in the early and middle 1600s. However, it is possible that Spanish, French, Italian and Portuguese traveled in or near the Hudson and Delaware River Valleys in the 1500s.[203] Henry Hudson "discovered" what is now the Hudson River in 1609. The initial relationship with the Dutch centered on trade—Lenape villagers exchanged fur and sometimes food for cooking utensils, guns and alcohol.[204] The Dutch eventually had interests in land, forming the New Amsterdam colony at present-day New York City in 1624 and Zwaanendael at the present-day town of Lewes, Delaware, in 1631. As the Dutch became more prevalent in the area, the Lenape suffered heavily from infectious diseases.[205] Early colonists wrote that many villages simply ceased[206] to exist, and by the "late 1650s, the lower Delaware Valley was probably a hotbed of infection that could have easily spread to Indians"[207] from the Dutch colonists.

From 1638 to 1655, the Swedes also established a colony along the Delaware River and christened it New Sweden. Like the Dutch, Swedish interests centered on fur. The colony was short-lived, however, having been incorporated into New Netherlands by 1655. Throughout this period, Lenape villagers would on occasion violently encounter their Swedish and Dutch neighbors, straining relations with the colonizers.[208] Historians describe several incidents of scalping, murder, robbery and other provocative actions arising from all sides.[209]

Diminished by the rapid expansion of European colonies and infectious disease, the Lenape faced an aggressive attempt from the neighboring Iroquois-speaking Susquehannock in the middle 1600s for dominance in the area's fur trade.[210] Both the Susquehannock and the northern Iroquois

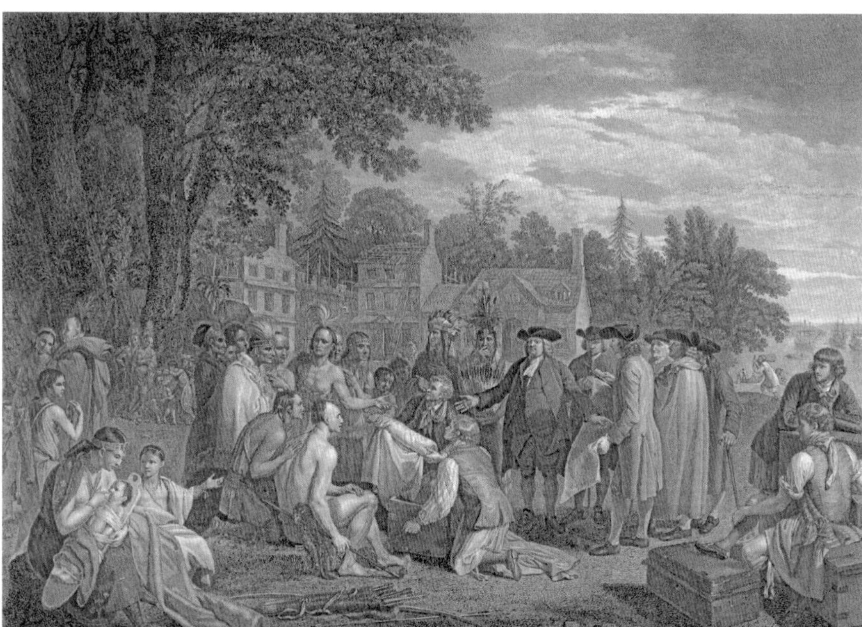

John Hall's depiction of William Penn signing a treaty with the Lenape. *Courtesy of the Library of Congress.*

Confederacy were harassing their southern neighbors for dominance in the fur trade.[211] C.A. Weslager wrote that Iroquois speakers were "roaming the Delaware Valley spreading terror."[212] The Iroquois attempt to dominate the fur trade during this period is contemporaneous with the Beaver War conflicts around the Great Lakes. While not every historian agrees, some suggest that the Iroquois subjugated the Lenape and had possibly "relegated the Delawares to the position of women, and in this role the Delawares were prohibited from going to war or negotiating treaties."[213]

Disease, warfare and European colonization began to push some of the Lenape peoples inland. While this most certainly changed social interactions, the "[f]lexibility toward land use and ownership aided the formation of alliances"[214] between the Lenape groups. During this same period, the Dutch and English fought two wars in which New Netherlands was contested. Changing hands a few times, the English eventually controlled the colony after the Treaty of Westminster in 1674, rechristening the New Amsterdam colony as New York.

Penn's Colony and the French and Indian War

By the year 1700, the British controlled the colonies up and down the Atlantic seaboard, with settlers pushing into the Appalachian Mountains. Lenape groups continued their dispersal west, but at a village, family and clan level. As there was no central authority, the move away from Europeans on the coast was haphazard. The Unami and Munsee speakers largely moved to two areas at "the Schuylkill [River] in the Delaware Valley, and many headed westward toward the Susquehanna [River]."[215] As the Lenape moved, different village bands forged new relationships and created unique identities. As Europeans pushed inland, they stole Native land under legal veneers, where Europeans held different concepts of land usage and ownership. The Dutch, Swedish and British saw land as something to legally possess, or own, where the Lenape saw land in terms of usage "in relation to its use and to the people utilizing it, more than as a passive object to be possessed and conceptualized apart from its function."[216] In short, when the Munsee and Unami villages entered land agreements with the Europeans, they "viewed land ownership in terms of usage rights, some of which were retained by the seller at the time of deeding."[217] In addition, since land was not "owned" by any one group of Lenape, "A specific territory might have been claimed in various ways by multiple owners,"[218] causing additional confusion among the British farmers, who came to believe that they "owned" the land after signing treaties. The British concept of ownership also included different habitation patterns, where it seemed to the Lenape that "the settlers were impelled by an urge to ruin the woods, the habitat of the birds and animals. It probably never occurred to the colonists, as they cut down the trees to obtain logs for buildings…and to make cleared land for pastures…that they were destroying the means by which the Indians obtained a livelihood."[219]

These different understandings of land aggravated the Lenape resettlement throughout the 1700s. William Penn's Quaker Colony put significant pressure on the Lenape in their ancestral home and at their new village sites near the Schuylkill and Susquehanna Rivers. Founded by charter in 1682, Penn began the colony immediately to the west of the Delaware River, pushing inland to an unknown western border. Penn "initiated and personally participated in a number of land purchases,"[220] and in doing so, he made sure that the various Lenape groups "clearly understood that *they were permanently conveying all ownership rights to him*. There was no longer any question of 'use' rights."[221] Penn had respect for the rights of the Lenape and treated them fairly, believing that the two could live together as equals.[222] Penn "held the confidence, respect, and friendship of the Delawares because his government gave the Indians a 'new deal.'"[223]

Throughout the early decades of the eighteenth century, both Unami and Munsee speakers moved farther west into Penn's colony, with additional settlements appearing along inland waterways. Who "owned" what and where became increasingly complex. The Pennsylvania authorities saw this land as legally owned by the white government, the Iroquois Confederacy saw western Pennsylvania Colony land as existing under their control and the French had interests piled near an ill-defined western border. Pennsylvania Colony territory became contested between French and English colonial powers, but the land itself saw pressure from excessive hunting and farming from all sides. The Lenape were caught in the middle. After Penn's death in 1718, his sons assumed control and were decidedly more hostile and less fair to the Lenape groups.[224] Throughout the first half of the eighteenth century, Pennsylvania colonists pushed the Lenape farther west, often engaging in fraudulent land dealings or resorting to outright violence.

The most notable dishonest land dealing occurred in the Pennsylvania Colony in 1737. Known as the Walking Purchase,[225] territorial officials came to Lenape elders with documents falsely suggesting that their ancestors had signed an agreement, giving away land "to the Penns…as much as could be covered in a day-and-a-half's walk."[226] Honor-bound, albeit under false pretenses, Lenape chief Lappawinsoe agreed to the arrangement under the impression that "the whites would take a leisurely walk down an Indian path along the Delaware River."[227] The Pennsylvania Colonial government hired three incredibly fast walkers who covered 5 miles in a day and half![228] The Lenape lost 1,200 square miles of land to the Pennsylvania Colony because of the deception.[229] The treacherous act removed the Lenape from the eastern part of the colony and turned many against the government, and "many of the Lenape sided with the French during the French and Indian War in order to strike back at the nation that had so betrayed them."[230]

By the time of the French and Indian War, many but not all Munsee and Unami speakers from the Susquehanna villages had moved to the Ohio River, south of present-day Pittsburgh. Many others stayed in the eastern part of the colony, and "[as] war broke out, western and eastern Delawares were in contact and influenced each other."[231] At the outset of the war, many Lenape remained neutral, opting to stay out of the conflict.[232] However, as the story spread of the Walking Purchase, coupled with the general British attitude of hostility toward the indigenous groups, the Lenape began favoring the French. The defeat of British general George Braddock at the Battle of the Monongahela by French and Native Americans and the surrender by George Washington at Fort Necessity also "resulted in complete alienation of Delawares and Shawnee on the Ohio."[233] By the end of the war however, both eastern and western groups of Lenape had "moved toward better relations with the British."[234] The Lenape leaders Teedyscung and Tamaqua worked toward producing a peaceful relationship with the British government.[235]

THE MORAVIAN MISSIONS AND LENAPE INFLUENCE ON PONTIAC

Throughout the eighteenth century, the Moravian Christians made several attempts to convert Lenape bands to Christianity. Often traveling with them as they relocated west, Moravians established missions among the Lenape in present-day Pennsylvania, Ohio and Indiana. Largely led by the efforts of David Zeisberger, the Moravians made strong inroads in converting Northern Unami and some Munsee speakers between the middle of the 1700s until the American Revolution. Zeisberger was well liked, having been adopted into the tribe in order to possess an influential seat on the Lupwaaeenóáuk.[236] Zeisberger's writings and observations have assisted in providing modern historians with a better understanding of the Lenape in the eighteenth century. Moravian missions were located throughout Pennsylvania Colony, and by the time of the American Revolution, several missions of Christian Lenape were located near present-day Coshocton, Ohio, at Gnadenhütten, Schoenbrunn, Salem and Lichtenau. A mission at Goshen, Ohio, was founded in 1798.

The Moravian missionaries were not entirely welcomed by all Lenape, an attitude that became more pronounced after the American Revolution. Disease and warfare continually played a part in keeping certain factions divided over issues of allegiance and religion; converts "fell under suspicion as a faction of Delawares disagreed with those who thought an association with the Moravians could help their people."[237] A series of Lenape "prophets" emerged at this time, urging followers to return to traditional ways of life. These prophets inaugurated nativist movements, with a message that "was clearly anti-white,"[238] blending various traditions. The "nativist revival may be interpreted not as an outgrowth of indigenous tradition, but rather as a basically European innovation expressed in native idiom."[239] The philologist Ray Whritenour added that these movements were "both a reactionary response to European religion and a revival of traditional forms of worship,"[240] a reflection of how both cultures influenced each other and modified their religious practices. This syncretic movement lasted through the later 1700s into the early 1800s and was centrally unorganized.[241]

One of the first prominent Lenape prophets was Neolin. In 1761, Neolin's visions compelled him to teach "the Indian had lost his 'avenue' to heaven by allowing the white man into his country and by adopting the white man's ways."[242] Neolin advocated for a return to traditional ways of living, foregoing trade with Europeans, alcohol, guns and a general refusal to "co-operate with white traders."[243] Neolin's teachings influenced many Lenape and other Native groups in the Ohio country, including Pontiac. Neolin was quite influential on Pontiac in the latter's rebellion.[244] While not all Lenape took part in Pontiac's Rebellion, many warriors were found with those who attacked the British. Around this same time, many bands moved west of Fort Pitt, into the present-day state of Ohio.[245] By the time of the American Revolution, Lenape groups had spread across Pennsylvania, New York and Ohio, with remnants still in New Jersey. The main body, consisting of both Munsee and Unami speakers, moved to the Tuscarawas River Valley, west of modern-day Pittsburgh at the present city of Coshocton, known to the Lenape as Koshaxkink.

THE AMERICAN REVOLUTION

The American Revolution was a divisive conflict for the Lenape. Literally caught between the American government in the east and British forces in the west, many Lenape originally settled on a position of neutrality. Attempting to be consistent with their mediator role as "Grandfathers" among the competing European powers and neighboring tribes, the Lenape leaders "found it difficult to resolve their differences and find consensus during the war."[246] While some warriors fought with the British, many Lenape "resisted providing outright military support for either side during the first few years of the war."[247]

The Lenape chief Koquethagechton (White Eyes) attempted to secure land for his Lenape band by signing the Treaty of Fort Pitt in 1778, the first official treaty between the American government and the Lenape. The treaty aligned the Lenape at Coshocton with the Americans in exchange for recognition of Lenape sovereignty.[248] The treaty promised the Lenape and their allies "to form a state whereof the Delaware nation shall be the head, and have a representation in Congress."[249] However, the Lenape were never unified in support of this treaty. Captain Pipe (Hopocan/Konieschquanoheel), a Wolf phratry war captain, and his warriors eventually supported the British, even though Pipe had signed the 1778 treaty.[250] The Turtle and Turkey phratries under White Eyes and Captain Killbuck (Gelelemend), respectively, "exhibited firm attachments to the Americans."[251] The result was that "Delaware neutralism gave way to a quarrelsome partisanship."[252]

At the conclusion of the treaty, White Eyes joined the American general Lachlan McIntosh on an expedition against the British at Detroit. During the trip, White Eyes was killed, and the American forces used smallpox as a cover for his murder. White Eyes' murder ended the loyalty toward the Americans held by sympathizing bands of Lenape.[253] At his death, Captain Pipe, Captain Killbuck, Buckhongehelas, Tetepachsit, Machingwe Pushis, Wingenund and Captain Johnny became prominent leaders;[254] many advocated for outright war against the Americans. With increasing numbers fighting with the British, the Americans sent commander Daniel Brodhead to the Coshocton area in April 1781. Brodhead's men destroyed the Coshocton village with the only remaining pro-American Lenape band under Killbuck. Brodhead's men suffered "no casualties during the campaign,"[255] with his Lenape allies under Killbuck "killing and scalping—a ruthless encounter of Delawares fighting Delawares."[256] At the request of

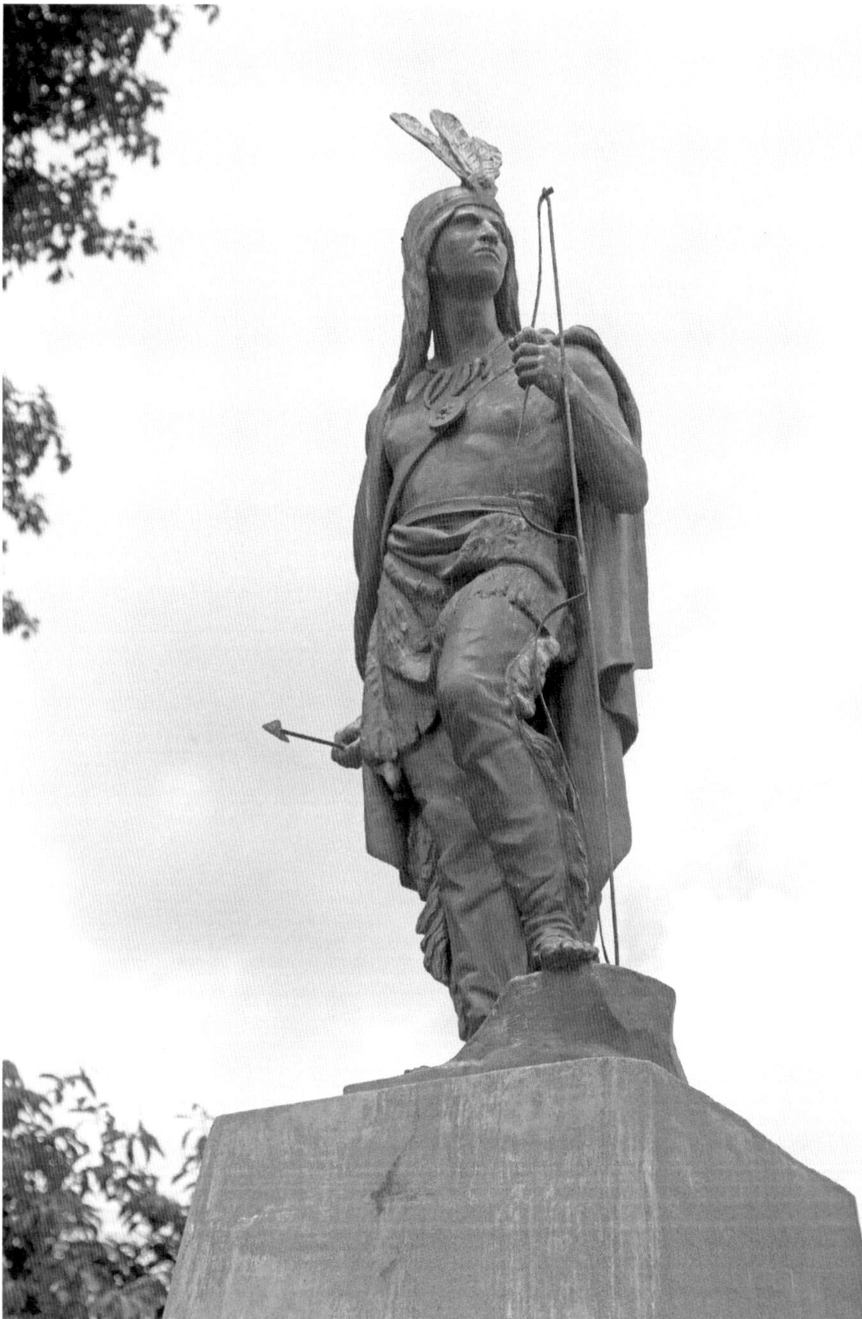

Statue of chief Captain Pipe (Hopocan) in Barberton, Ohio. *Author's collection.*

the Moravian missionaries, Brodhead left the Moravian Lenape alone and marched back to Fort Pitt. Soon after, a band of pro-British Lenape, led by Chief Buckhongehelas, visited the villagers at Gnadenhütten and warned them to be wary of the "long knives" (Americans) and that the previous attack at Coshocton should be "sufficient warning to you; and to lead you to consult your own safety."[257] Later in the year, the Moravian Lenape were moved to the Upper Sandusky River near Lake Erie at Captive Town, where they remained for the winter. Nearly starving, the Moravian groups were allowed to return to their villages in the following spring to gather supplies and food.

In early March, Lieutenant Colonel David Williamson of the American Pennsylvania militia marched into Gnadenhütten to respond to an erroneous report that the Lenape there had attacked people living in western Pennsylvania. Leading a raiding party of 160 militiamen, Williamson's group "blamed the Christian Indians they found there for having taken part in the raids, which was untrue."[258] Known today as the Gnadenhütten Massacre, Williamson's men voted to execute the villagers on March 8, all of whom were noncombatants. The Moravian Lenape, knowing their fate, requested the night for prayer. As dawn broke the following morning, Williamson's men pulled the Lenape converts—most were children, women and elderly men—into two cabins,

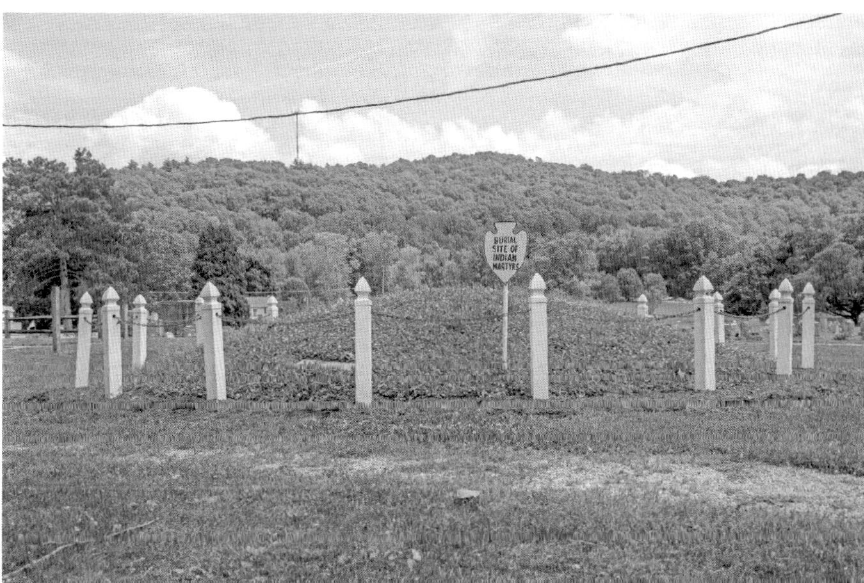

Grave site of Gnadenhutten Massacre victims. *Author's collection.*

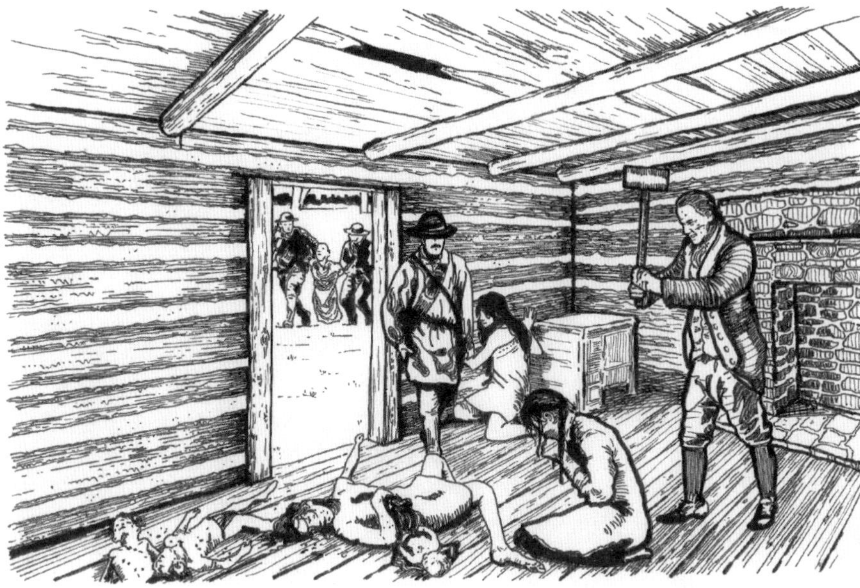

Artist's depiction of the Gnadenhütten Massacre in March 1782. *Courtesy of George Everett Keller.*

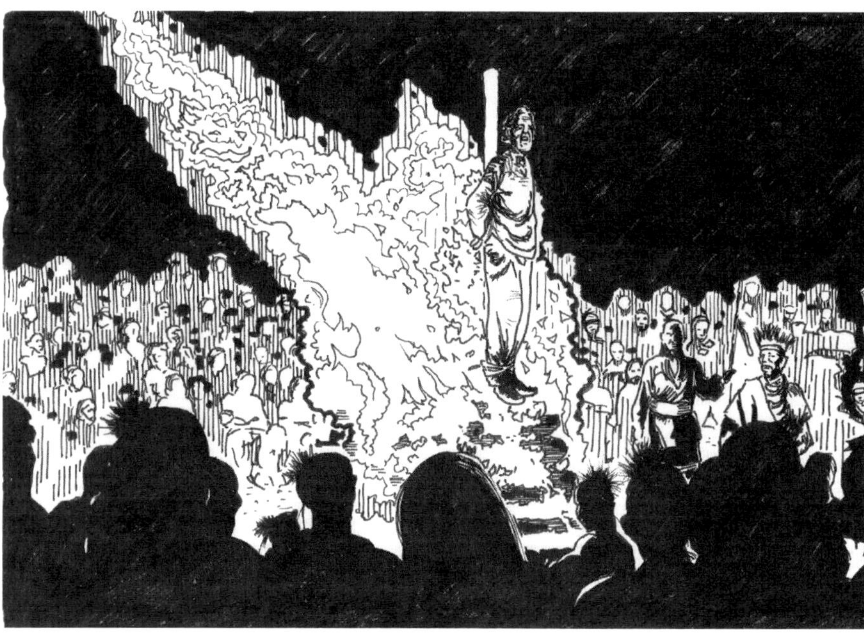

The execution of William Crawford as retaliation for the Gnadenhütten Massacre in June 1782. *Courtesy of George Everett Keller.*

and they "were beaten to death with mallets and hatchets, and scalped"[259] as they sang Christian hymns and pleaded for their lives. The militia murdered "56 adult Indians…29 men, 27 women, and 34 children of various ages—a total of 90 victims. The militiamen returned with 96 scalps—they must have killed unconverted Indians somewhere along their route."[260] Several prominent Lenape leaders were killed in the massacre, including Welapachtschiechen, Glikhikan and Netanewand.[261] A young boy escaped by hiding in the floor of one of the buildings, later saying that "the blood flowed in the house like a river."[262] Sometime later, the Moravian missionary John Heckwelder gathered the remains of those murdered and buried them in a mound near the site of the massacre.

The massacre at Gnadenhütten deeply affected all of the Lenape in the Ohio country. With a population at this time of only a few thousand, ninety deaths were felt across all Lenape bands. Some sought revenge. In June 1782, Captain Pipe (Hopocan/Konieschquanoheel) captured an American militia commander, Colonel William Crawford, and burned him at the stake to "avenge the massacre at Gnadenhütten."[263] Williamson, however, "was never taken by the Indians, nor was he tried in a white man's court for the crime."[264]

Northwest Indian War

After the American Revolution, the tribes in the Ohio country looked on the new American government with concern. The British signed away their rights to the land south of the Great Lakes over to the Americans "without the feeblest attempt to protect the rights of its undefeated Indian allies who occupied much of the region."[265] The United States government sought to utilize the land for white settlement, despite thousands of Natives in residence. The many tribes along the western frontier strengthened their commitments to each other, and "despite the boasting of American commissioners that they had conquered the Indian tribes in the Revolution, the United States government and not the Indian alliances steadily weakened through the 1780s."[266] Forming a loose alliance known as the Western Confederacy, the Miami, Wyandot, Lenape, Kickapoo, Wabash Confederation, Potawatomi, Ojibwe, Odawa, Kaskaskia and Lower Cherokee organized to harass and prevent the settlement of the Northwest Territory. This was the second great alliance

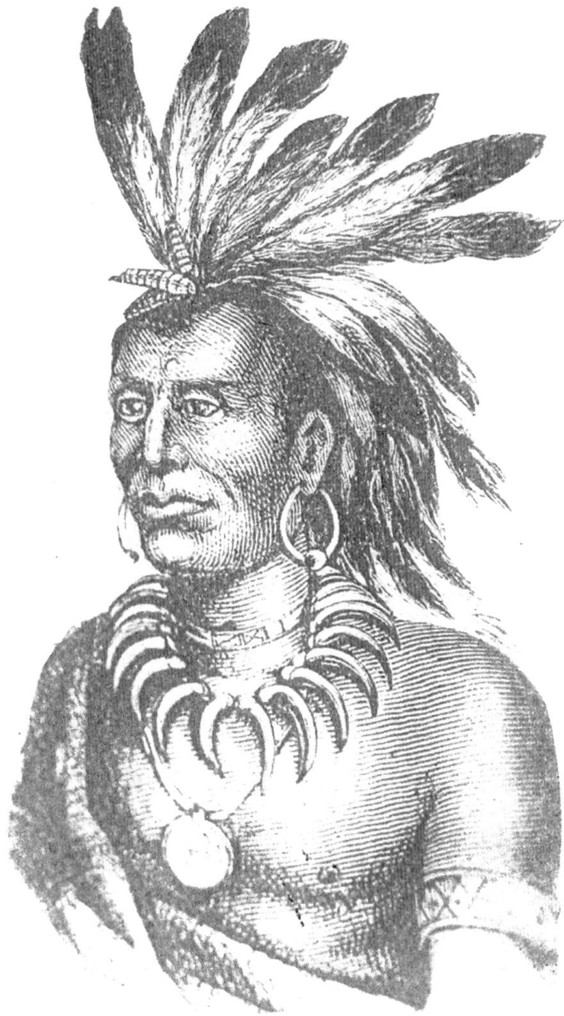

Rendering of Miami chief Little Turtle, in John Dillon's *History of Indiana*.

of mostly Algonquian-speaking peoples against white encroachment. The primary leaders of the Western Confederacy were the Miami chief Little Turtle, the Shawnee chief Blue Jacket and the Lenape chief Buckhongehelas. While many Lenape did not fight, several bands sent warriors who took part in major conflicts.

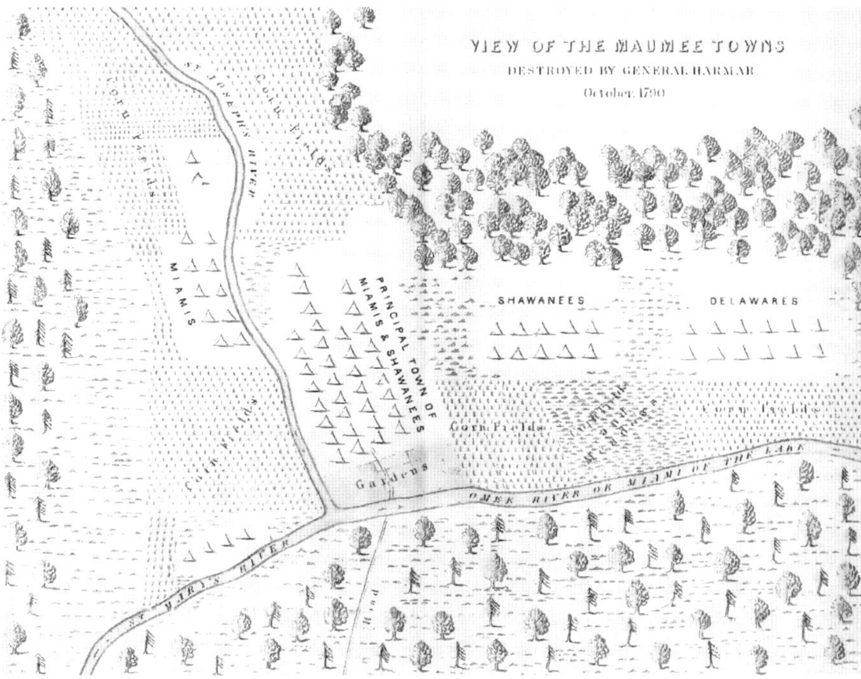

1790 Map depicting Kekionga. *Courtesy of Wikicommons.*

As discussed previously, after the defeat of American forces under Harmar and St. Clair, Anthony Wayne concluded the Northwest Indian War at the Battle of Fallen Timbers, forcing the tribes to cede their Ohio country territory at the signing of the Treaty of Greenville in 1795. At this time, the main body of Lenape had no home, with bands spread across the eastern United States from Pennsylvania through Ohio, southern Canada and southern Indiana. In Trowbridge's interviews, he found that "the great body of the nation removed to Fort Wayne, where they remained until Harmer's defeat, when they moved from the ashes of their village to a place about 12 miles above Defiance. Here they [stayed] a short time and then removed to the Auglaize,"[267] where they stayed until the end of the Northwest Indian War. Eventually, they "removed to their old stand above Defiance on the Maumee, where they remained until the treaty of Greenville."[268]

The Miamis invited the Lenape to live along the two forks of the White River in their territory. The main Lenape body accepted the offer, establishing villages along the west fork in east-central Indiana near present-day Muncie, downriver into present-day Marion County. Other bands of Lenape moved back to the Coshocton area, and still others lived near the Sandusky River with the Wyandot. Another group of Lenape had moved from the Ohio country to Spanish Cape Girardeau along the Mississippi River in 1793. This group eventually moved into present-day Texas, ultimately residing in western Oklahoma. As bands of Lenape and affiliated groups spread across the new country and into Canada by the early 1800s, "though widely dispersed [they] maintained connections across long distances and forged alliances with new neighbors."[269] Several groups moved to what is now Canada, where they remain today.

Chapter 7

The White River Lenape

Controlled by the Miami as a hunting ground, the land between the east and west forks of the White River was largely uninhabited when the Lenape resettled after the Northwest Indian War. While neither fork possessed enough water for consistently easy travel, the area did have a strong network of trails. The White River watershed held sufficient amounts of fish, and the adjacent forests had ample game. The river valleys provided rich soil, attracting both American and Native farmers. The prominent Miami villages existed to the north and west along the Wabash River, but smaller settlements were located immediately north of the west fork of the White River along the Mississinewa River. Shawnee were scattered nearby across southern Indiana and Ohio. As we shall see, prominent Shawnee leaders occasionally lived near the Lenape. The Moravian missionaries in Indiana speak of Cherokee, Wyandot, Miami, Shawnee, Piankashaw and Wea passing through the area. An affiliated band of Nanticoke also moved with the Lenape, establishing a village near present-day Anderson. By the late 1810s, Brotherton Native Americans, or "York Indians," had moved to the river just as the main body of Lenape moved west. The missionaries also indicated that east-central Indiana possessed white traders, French Canadian trappers and free men of African descent. The missionaries themselves were German, rendering the early 1800s White River Valley a truly diverse region. Along with the three Moravian missionaries, John and William Conner lived and traded with the Lenape. Each brother married a member of the tribe, maintaining strong relationships between both worlds.

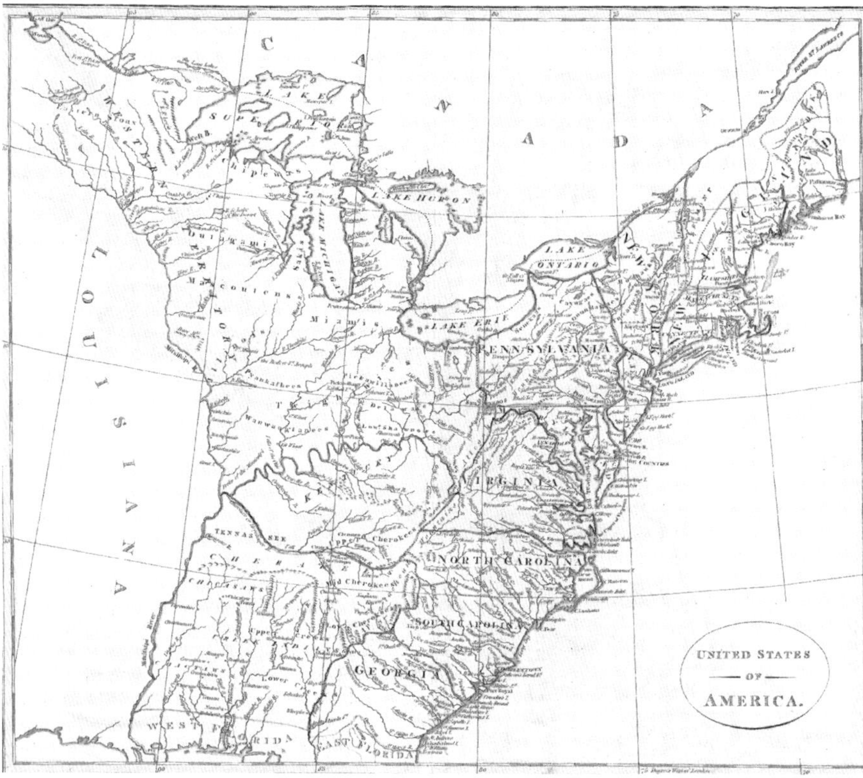

Clement Crutwell's 1799 map of America. *Courtesy of the Library of Congress.*

Even though the Lenape strived for solidification of their identity in Indiana, by the time they reached the White River, their lives had been shattered. From the time of permanent Dutch settlement in the 1600s until their arrival on the White River in the 1790s, Unami and Munsee speakers had been scattered across the entire western frontier from the Appalachians to the Northwest Territory. They had seen their population drop significantly from disease and had participated in every major military conflict. A band of Moravian Lenape had been massacred during the American Revolution. Alcoholism, frontier violence, anger, territorial disputes, and white encroachment continued to plague the bands at this time. As they coalesced into Indiana, tribal leaders made efforts to bring all of the Unami and Munsee speakers together on the White River. While many Lenape did move to the Indiana Territory, several bands did not, remaining permanently separated.

The Lenape were living in land controlled or "owned" by Miami. While the indigenous tribes firmly understood Euro-American concepts of landownership by the late 1700s, Euro-American and Native groups would often quarrel over the "legal" owner of the land. The United States government held the view that the Northwest Territory had been ceded to the new nation at the end of the Revolution, while tribes legally owned title to specific tracts of land. The government's policies aimed to either convert the indigenous inhabitants to settle the land as whites did or to sell their territory and move west of the Mississippi River. Thomas Jefferson "called upon all Americans to cooperate in teaching the natives agriculture and the domestic arts to help change their status from huntsmen to farmers and artisans."[270] This rarely happened, and while it is certain that some Lenape, Miami and Wea stayed behind, all tribes in Indiana eventually moved west. In the end, the key point remains that the Lenape were living on Miami land in a politically organized American territory identified as "Indiana"—land of the Indians. We do not fully understand the exact Miami-Lenape arrangement, as the "whole subject of lands allocated by the Miami is not well understood because no written leases changed hands, and no surveyor's drawings were made to show the bounds of tracts the Miami assigned to the newcomers."[271] The signing of early treaties in Indiana by Lenape chiefs caused occasional friction with their Miami hosts, as the Miami saw themselves as legal owners of the land.

Settlements Along the River

Prior to the 1790s, the Piankashaw had invited a smaller Lenape band living in Ohio to settle in southern Indiana, near the confluence of both east and west forks of the White River and the Wabash River in the 1760s.[272] We know far less about the southern Indiana Lenape than their east-central counterparts. We do know that in 1779, a band of these southern Indiana Lenape had allegedly "killed and plundered"[273] a few white hunters. George Rogers Clark dispatched rangers, who attacked them "without delay—their camps were attacked in every quarter where they could be found; many fell, and others were brought to Post Vincennes and put to death; the women and children secured, etc."[274] The extent these southern Indiana Lenape communicated with their east-central counterparts is not known.

With this exception, the main body of the Lenape, mostly Unami speakers with some Munsee bands, had moved to several villages along the west fork of the White River by 1796. These villages stretched from the south of present-day Muncie downriver to just inside present-day Marion County.[275] There were as many as fourteen separate villages, some more prominent than others. A few were seasonal trading camps, and not all fourteen existed at the same time. The sources are also unclear as to their exact locations, although we have a decent idea approximately where they were situated on the river. Many Hoosiers erroneously think that the Native word for the west fork of the White River is *Wahapahni*, but this is incorrect.[276] The Lenape referred to the river as *Opeecomecah*, and the Miami called the west fork *Waapikaminki*.[277] The Unami word for a white river is *opeksipu*. Early French maps identify the river as *la riviere Blanche* and *Maison blanche*.[278]

The fourteen villages along *Opeecomecah* include: 1) Wapicomekoke, Buckhongehelas' Town or Old Town; 2) Munsee Town, Tetepachsit's Town or Wapicomekunk; 3) the York Indian Village; 4) Hockingpomsga's Town, or Owenachki; 5) Killbuck's Village, or Buck's Town; 6) the Moravian Mission, Mission Town, Little Munsee Town, Wapiminischikeck or Wapimintschi; 7) Anderson's Town, or Wapiminskink; 8) Nancy's Town, or the Nanticoke Village; 9) Greentown; 10) Strawtown; 11) Sarah's Town; 12) Upper Delaware Town; 13) Connerstown, or Conner's Trading Post; and 14) Lower Delaware Town, or Brouillette's Village.[279] The specific names are often in dispute among historians, cartographers, missionaries and early settlers. The primary evidence is simply not reliable. There may have been more villages or fewer, but the record seems to indicate at least fourteen established locations. The great Shawnee leader Tecumseh; his brother, Lalawethika (Tenskwatawa/the Prophet); and their band of Shawnee established a summer village along the White River for a brief period, locating "his new town a little northwest of present-day Anderson, close to the line between Hamilton and Madison Counties."[280] They lived here seasonally from about 1798 until 1806.[281] It is not uncommon to see references suggesting that Tecumseh and his brother lived at Buckhongehelas' Town for a time, although this is unlikely.

A local legend also suggests that the famous Lenape captain Pipe (Hopocan/Konieschquanoheel) lived with the White River Lenape for a time in the late 1810s and had a village near Orestes—a few miles north of the river. Trowbridge is recorded having met with *a* Captain Pipe (probably Tahunqueecoppi),[282] but it might have been a son or nephew to Hopocan. However, there simply is no evidence that *the* Captain Pipe (Hopocan) was ever in Indiana, having probably remained with a Lenape band in Ohio. His name never appears in any of the Lenape treaties during their time in Indiana, and Hopocan likely died in the 1790s.

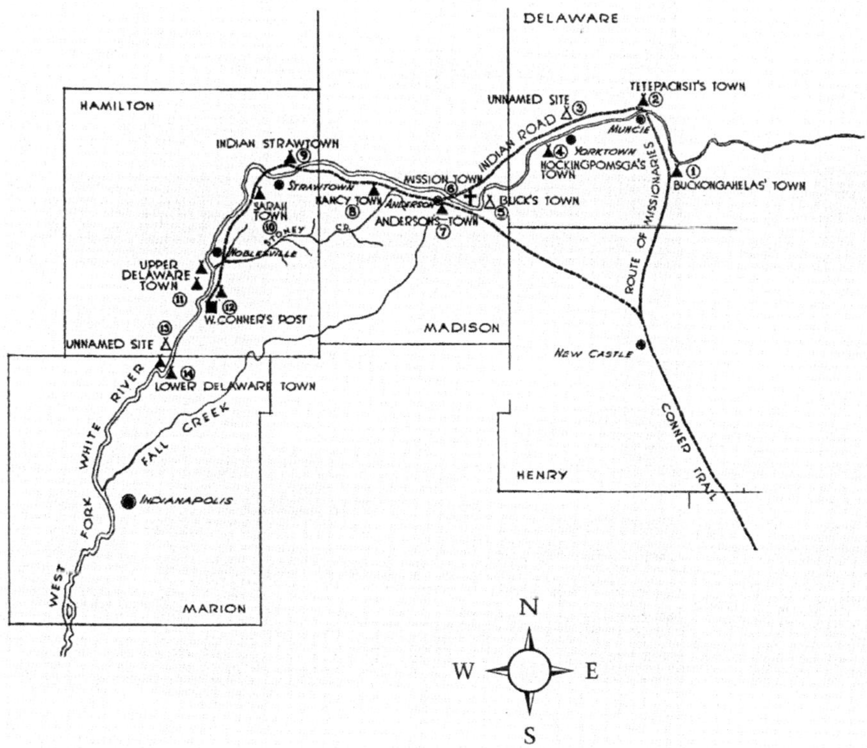

INDIAN TOWNS NEAR MORAVIAN MISSION AND CONNER TRAIL

Approximate locations of the White River Lenape villages. *Courtesy of Conner Prairie Interactive History Park.*

Suffice it to say, the most prominent villages included the following:[283]

- Buckhongehelas' Town also appears as Wapicomikoke, Wapicamikunk, Old Town and Utenink. When the Lenape first moved to the White River, their most venerable chief was Buckhongehelas. His town was located a few miles south of the present-day city of Muncie. This served as the principal village during the early years until Buckhongehelas's death and perhaps after. John Conner lived here for a time as well. It is possible that the inhabitants abandoned or largely left the town at some point. Early white settlers knew it as "Old Town."

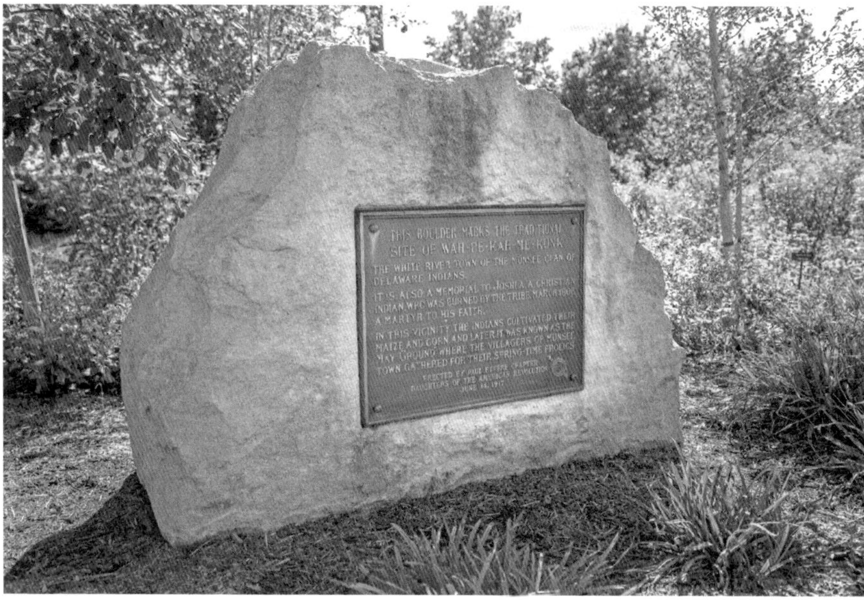

Marker placed near the site of Tetepachsit's Village (Munsee Town/Wapicamikunk). *Author's collection.*

- MUNSEE TOWN served as the principal town of Munsee speakers. At times, it was referred to as New Town or Tetepachsit's Town—named after the chief who lived there—and also, confusingly, as Wapicamikunk. The town was located just north of the White River bend in present-day Muncie, along or at Minnetrista Boulevard.

- HOCKINGPOMSGA'S VILLAGE was the village site of Chief Hockingpomsga. The town is also referred to as Owenachki. We do not know much about this town, but it was probably located near Priest Ford Road, just west of the present-day town of Yorktown on or near the property of the Kilgore farm.[281] Hockingpomsga was involved in the black market whiskey trade.

- MORAVIAN MISSION was the mission of John Kluge, Anna Kluge and Abraham Luckenbach from 1801 to 1806. While it was never as large as the Moravian Lenape missions out east, the missionaries did have several Lenape with them in Indiana. After the missionaries left in 1806, the Lenape may have lived in the vicinity at a village identified as Lower Munsee Town. The site is also referred to as Wapimintschi.

- Anderson's Town was the village site of Chief William Anderson (Kikthawenund). By the time the Lenape left, Chief Anderson had become the prominent chief, so it is logical to conclude that his town grew in preeminence as the years progressed. Anderson's Town is generally believed to be at or near the site of the Madison County Courthouse.

- The Nanticoke Village is sometimes referred to as Nantico, or Nancy's town. While the population of this village was never high, it is significant because it was home to a Nanticoke band, an affiliated tribe that traveled with the Lenape.

- Conner's Trading Post was the home of William Conner. After living with Kikthawenund, Conner married his daughter Mekinges ("muh-kun-jis") and moved to the site to begin a trading operation. While never a village, the site was home to the Conner/Mekinges family, and many Lenape would set camp at or near the trading post. The Lenape all gathered here to live for a short while before moving on to Missouri in 1821. The site is located in Fishers and is currently home to the Conner Prairie Interactive Museum.

The other villages most likely were smaller trading posts, seasonal villages or the settlements of small family units. The sources simply do not agree, and many of the sites have similar names, or the same name, further magnifying the difficulty in understanding. The exact population of Lenape living along the White River at this time is unknown. Weslager has it that "before the removal across the Mississippi, there were probably about two thousand persons in the main body of Delawares living at Piqua and along the White River, but this figure by no means constituted the total Delaware Indian population."[285]

PROMINENT CHIEFS

As Trowbridge indicated in his interviews with Captain Pipe (Tahunqueecoppi, Hopocan's nephew or son), the Lenape governed with three civilian chiefs and three war chiefs, answerable to the council of wise men known as the Lupwaaaeenóáuk.[286] By the time the Lenape settled on the White River, several prominent men had become leaders, including the venerable war chief Buckhongehelas, Hockingpomsga, Tetepachsit (the Grand Glaize King) and Kikthawenund (William Anderson). When the Lenape left Indiana, Kikthawenund had become *the* prominent chief, the others having died from disease, old age or in the internal purges that took place in 1806. Other chiefs reported during this time include Amochk (the Beaver), Petchekekapon, Captain Killbuck (perhaps son of the famous Killbuck/Gelelemend), Lapahnihe (Big Bear), James Nanticoke, White Eyes (relative of the famous Lenape White Eyes), Quenaghtoothmait, Captain Tunis and others.

Buckhongehelas was revered as "the George Washington of the Delawares"[287] by the Lenape at the time and was a celebrated warrior, having fought in many battles throughout his life. He also warned the Lenape at Gnadenhütten before the massacre and continually held a hostile stance toward whites and Christianity, as he was "a

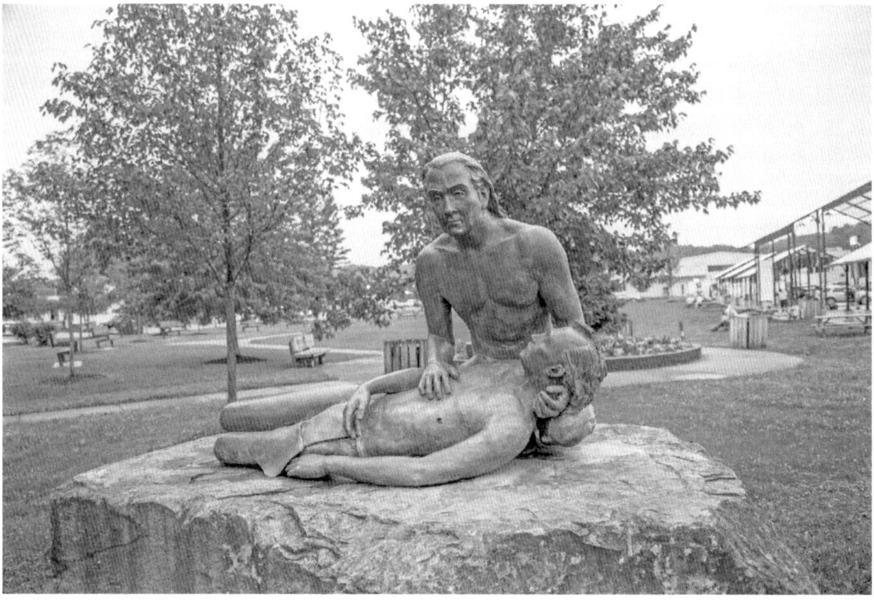

Bill Hopen's sculpture of Buckhongehelas in Buckhannon, West Virginia. *Author's collection.*

hardened pagan, strongly opposed to the conversion of his people to Christianity."[288] He possessed "a great amount of shrewdness combined with unusual oratorical ability [making] him an influential factor among the Indians."[289] In 1787, Buckhongehelas once warned his people that "there are good white men, but they bear no proportion to the bad; the bad must be the strongest, for they rule,"[290] concluding his speech with, "Remember that this day I have warned you to beware of such friends as these. I know the long knives; they are not to be trusted."[291] The great chief died in 1806 of either influenza or smallpox.

In the early years, Tetepachsit, known as the Grand Glaize King, also led the White River Lenape. He was the principal chief at Munsee Town and "was the head of the nation"[292] as a chief first among equals. In terms of personality, he was "a quiet, inoffensive and harmless man of sixty or more"[293] with a "fairly good character and had as such the best interests of his people at heart."[294] To offset his "good character," he would on occasion carry "with him a string of twenty-seven dried human tongues which he proudly offered as a grim and mute testimony that he was not a weakling."[295] Tetepachsit was marked as a "witch" and executed by the tribe in 1806, with his son delivering a blow to the head with a tomahawk. Hockingpomsga was "renowned as a witch-doctor. He was not only given to drink but dealt in whiskey and derived from this nefarious traffic his only source of income,"[296] having become a successor to Captain Pipe (Hopocan), further suggesting that Hopocan had died in the 1790s and could not have lived with the White River Lenape.[297] Hockingpomsga, too, was identified as a witch during the purges of 1806, but narrowly escaped execution. His ultimate fate is unknown.

By the time they left Indiana, Kikthawenund had become the preeminent chief of the White River Lenape. Although a chief at the signing of the Treaty of Greenville, Kikthawenund's early role was minimal. However, he rose in prominence throughout the three decades in Indiana, successfully navigating his people through difficulty. Kikthawenund was born in the 1750s to a Swedish ferryboat operator on the Susquehanna River and a Lenape mother, who may have been the daughter of the Lenape chief Netawatawees.[298] Kikthawenund's daughter Mekinges married William Conner, forging an alliance between the chief and trader. Kikthawenund's "stature grew following Buckongahelas's death, although he did not actually become the principal chief until the death of Tetepachsit."[299] He was also the principal leader of the Turkey phratry.[300]

Kikthawenund was a formidable man who "was a very dignified man in character and appearance, upward of six feet tall, well proportioned, a man of great benevolence and power, of excellent understanding, but not a great speaker."[301] In the early 1820s, Kikthawenund lead the Lenape west first to Missouri and then on into Kansas, dying in 1831.[302] He had many children, and his descendants appear throughout Lenape tribal history in Kansas and Oklahoma. The significance of his legacy, beyond progeny, lies with Kikthawenund's ability to keep the Lenape largely out of the Shawnee Prophet's nativist movement, Tecumseh's War and the War of 1812.

TREATIES

Almost immediately after the Lenape moved to the White River, Indiana territorial governor William Henry Harrison worked to promote white settlement. Territorial officials sought either to extinguish the Native Americans' title in Indiana or to settle them as farmers. Harrison offered the Lenape "farm implements, plows, and oxen at reasonable prices, and men were sent to teach them how to fence their cultivated fields."[303] The Lenape resisted many of these efforts and were simply "not ready to give up their activity in the woods and along the streams to allow the white men to turn them into dirt farmers."[304] Harrison was patient for a time "in the hope of civilizing them, but if that failed to remove them beyond the Mississippi."[305]

Between the Treaty of Greenville in 1795 and the Treaty of St. Mary's in 1818, the tribe's chiefs signed away significant amounts of territory, mostly in southern Indiana. Many of these treaties and agreements were signed in the first decade of the 1800s.[306] As the Lenape did not legally own any of the land in Indiana, the Piankashaw and Miami became enraged when Lenape signatures appeared on treaties, giving away land they did not own legally. Lenape marks appear on agreements at Vincennes, Grouseland and Fort Wayne in the first decade and again in 1809, when the Indiana government received "about two million nine hundred thousand acres of land"[307] from the Lenape, Potawatomi, Miami and Eel River Miami. Most of this land was in southern Indiana. The news was not always received well by tribal members on the White River. While the ceded territory was not

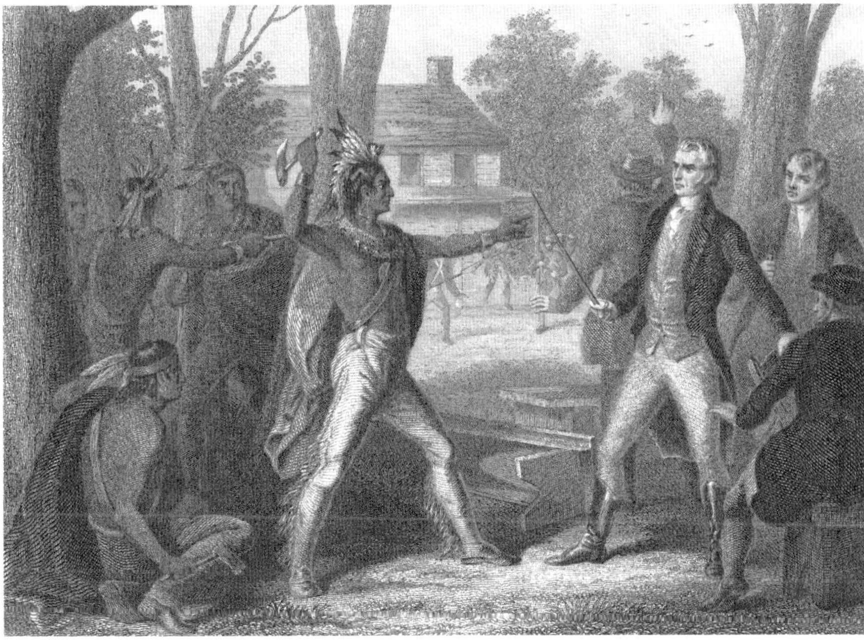

Above: Depiction of a tense meeting between Tecumseh and William Henry Harrison in 1810. *Courtesy of the Indiana Historical Society (P0483).*

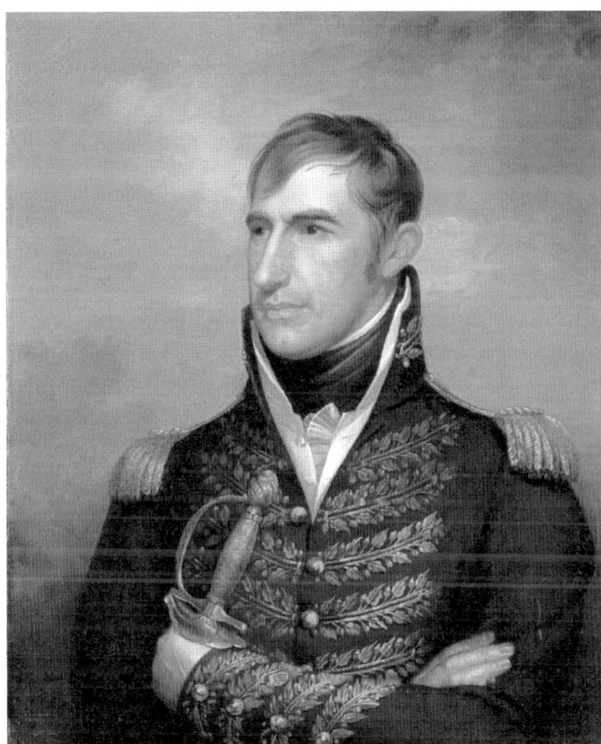

Right: Rembrandt Peale's 1813 portrait of William Henry Harrison. *Wikicommons.*

necessarily inhabited, it represented a reduction of hunting grounds, which ultimately diminished the food supply and sources of fur.[308] Some of the senior chiefs became caught in an internal purge in 1806 because "there was increasing evidence that the senior chiefs were not performing their duties"[309] and did not have the Lenape's best interests in dealing with the territorial government.

Chapter 8

The Moravians and the Conners

While white traders and trappers would pass through the camps, very few people of European descent were found along the White River at this time. The most prominent were John and William Conner, traders who at first lived at Lenape villages before establishing posts of their own, and the Moravian missionaries John Kluge, Anna Kluge and Abraham Luckenbach. The Kluges later had a son at the mission named John. The

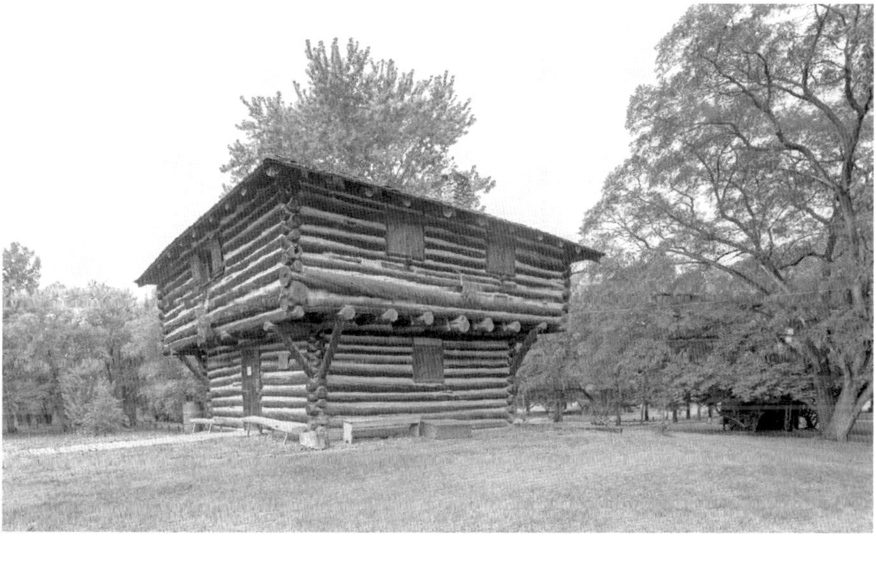

Re-creation of an early blockhouse at Fort Ouiatenon near Lafayette. *Author's collection.*

missionaries' diaries also mention several Frenchmen—most likely French Canadians remaining or descended from the French period that lived, traded and married among the White River Lenape.[310] During the 1810s, records indicate that an increasing number of white settlers began moving into areas south of east-central Indiana. Militia troops also had semi-permanent camps in the area during the War of 1812. A series of "forts" or blockhouses were "constructed from Vincennes to Greenville"[311] and most likely existed on both branches of the White River.[312]

JOHN AND WILLIAM CONNER

The Conner brothers[313] had an intimate history with the Lenape throughout much of their lives. Both brothers had lived with the Lenape and their parents in the Ohio country. After moving to Michigan, the brothers' father, Richard, established a farm near Detroit. This frontier experience rendered both Conners fluent in Munsee and Unami. Their upbringing in the Ohio frontier and their fluency in Lenape languages—but possibly also German, Shawnee, Chippewa and Wyandot—allowed them to communicate freely in the frontier.

After their father's death, both brothers inherited his property and the income derived from it but "definitely rejected a settled agricultural existence for the freer and more exciting life of the Indian trader."[314] William and John became agents for a fur trader and had settled with the White River Lenape by 1801. Their exact movements in the early years are not entirely known, but we do know that John lived at Buckhongehelas' Town and William with Kikthawenund. John and William's sympathetic outlook and respect for the Lenape, along with their Unami fluency, earned admiration from the Lenape. "The Delawares, especially, trusted these two traders to a greater extent than any other white men."[315] The Conners both married Lenape women, with William marrying Kikthawenund's daughter Mekinges. Both brothers "not only wore the dress of the Indians but had adopted their manners, spiritual views, and ways of thoughts."[316] However, they never became "thoroughly Indian in character, outlook, and interests."[317]

John Conner eventually established a store near the Big Cedar Grove Creek in the Whitewater River Valley and later founded the city of Connersville in present-day Fayette County. William Conner left Anderson's Town and established a trading post near present-day Fishers.

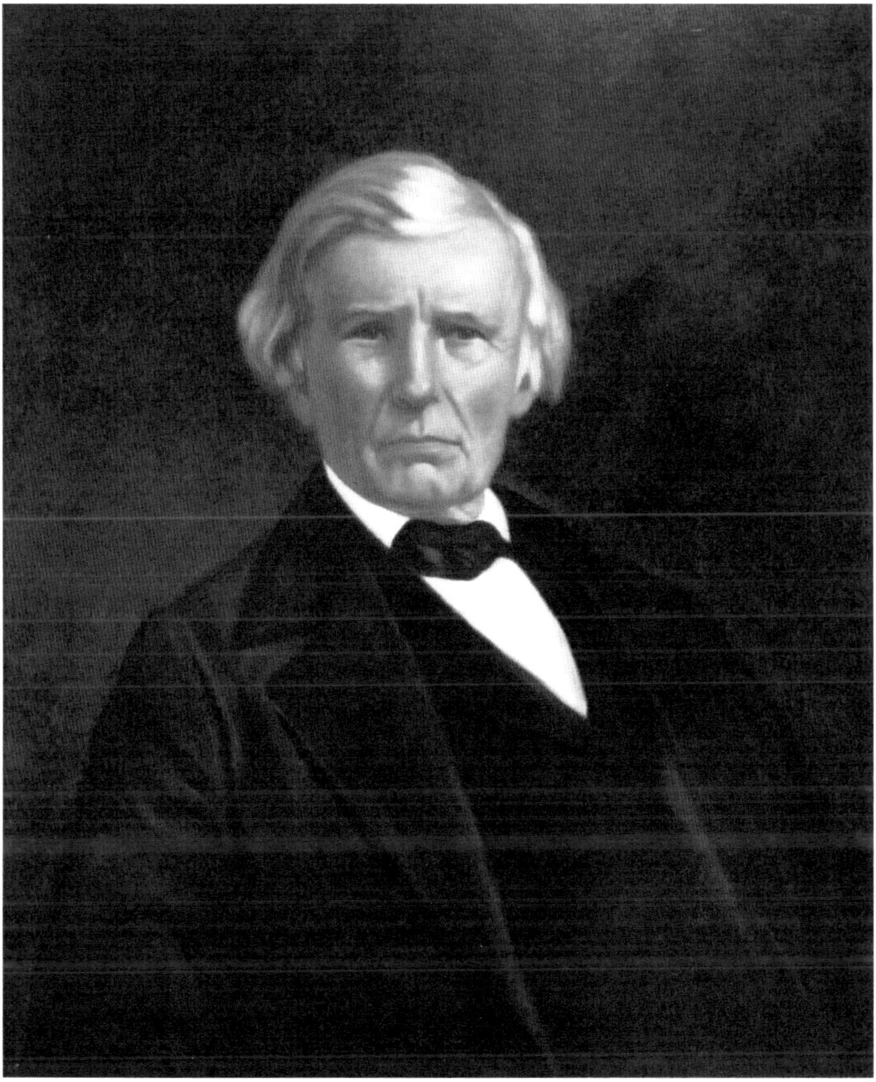

Portrait of William Conner. *Courtesy of Conner Prairie Interactive History Park.*

The Conners continued to serve as traders, scouts, fixers, negotiators and territorial statesmen in the early decades of the 1800s. William traveled with American forces during the War of 1812, having perhaps identified Tecumseh's body after he was killed at the Battle of Thames.[318] When the tribe left, both Conner wives went west, leaving John and William to become significantly involved in Indiana's transition from a territory to state. While there is no record that either Conner ever saw his first wife or children again, prominent Lenape with "Conner" surnames appear throughout later tribal history.

THE MORAVIAN MISSION

We know a fair amount of history about the White River Lenape in the early years due to the diaries of the Moravian missionaries. While the Moravians only stayed briefly, their documentation of the events from 1801 to 1806 provide modern historians with ample first-person accounts of events. For the sake of brevity, this chapter will only highlight the main story of the mission and their interactions with their Lenape neighbors.

The Moravian mission was established among the White River Lenape in part by miscommunication, or perhaps plain arrogance on behalf of the missionaries. The Moravian missionary David Zeisberger had suggested that a mission should be established along the White River. The Moravians reached out to the tribal council with that request. The Lenape replied with an invitation for the converts to join them in Indiana, but the "moravian missionaries were not specifically included in the invitation nor was there any longing expressed for the gospel."[319] As they had done in Ohio, the White River Lenape chiefs were simply looking to bring together "the scattered bands of their tribe in order to strengthen their position."[320] It is unclear if the Moravians understood this and disregarded or if they were under the impression that their accompaniment was implicit with the invitation to the Christian Lenape.

Regardless, by 1800, the decision had been made to establish a mission along the White River. In late 1800, Brother Abraham Luckenbach; Brother John Kluge; his wife, Sister Anna Kluge; a Mahican convert named Joshua; and a small band of Lenape converts started the journey to the White. In the fall of that year, the group moved from Bethlehem, Pennsylvania, to Goshen in Ohio—both prominent Moravian centers. They traveled through southern Ohio and then up the southeastern side of Indiana until they reached Buckhongehelas' Town in May 1801. From there, they traveled to a site where they established a mission village and named it Woapimintshi, meaning "the place near the chestnut tree." The mission town was located between Killbuck's village and Anderson's Town on the eastern edge of present-day Anderson. For the next five years, the missionaries worked very hard to establish their

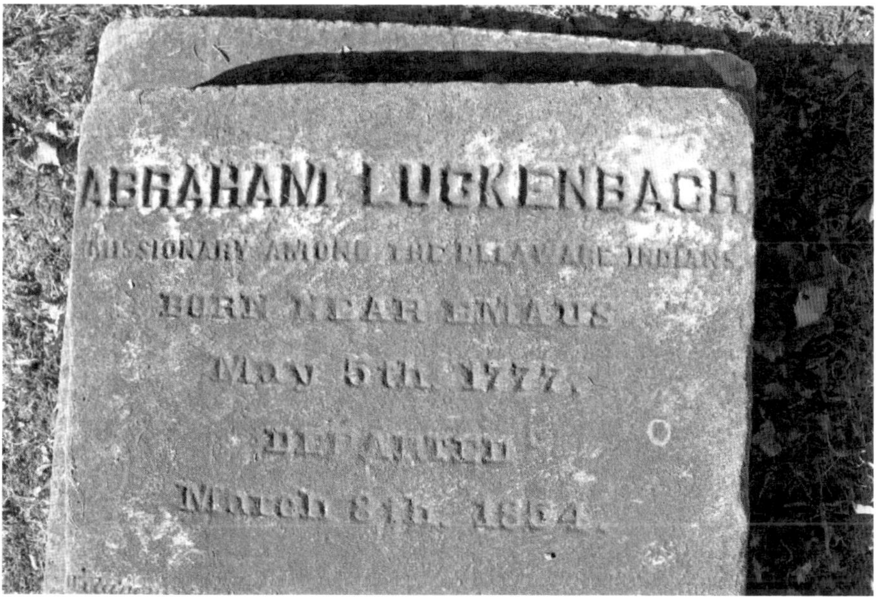

Grave marker of Moravian missionary Abraham Luckenbach. *Courtesy of Leo Caldwell.*

mission with houses, farms and maple syrup camps—attempting to make inroads with their Lenape neighbors and hoping to win converts.

The missionaries never converted many Lenape. Only a few individual families stayed the entire time, with most staying for a few weeks at best, eventually returning to their villages. The most prominent Native villager was a Mahican convert named Joshua. Joshua appears many times in the diaries and had a positive relationship with the Moravians. While the diaries express chagrin that he drank whiskey and caroused with women, he remained a stalwart at Mission Town until his death. He did have a troubled life. Two of his daughters were murdered at Gnadenhütten and several other offspring died from disease. He "led an uneasy existence, caught between native and Moravian worlds. Although his talents ranged from that of musician and translator to skilled handyman, his life was filled with grief and discord during three marriages."[321] The missionaries relied heavily on his farming and carpentry skills.

The diaries should always be read with the understanding that the Moravians had a Christian, Euro-American-centric, biased view. However, the diaries do yield a wealth of information about life in east-central Indiana, referring to consistently devastating waves of disease affecting both whites and Natives. The diaries suggest that the area bustled with peoples from different

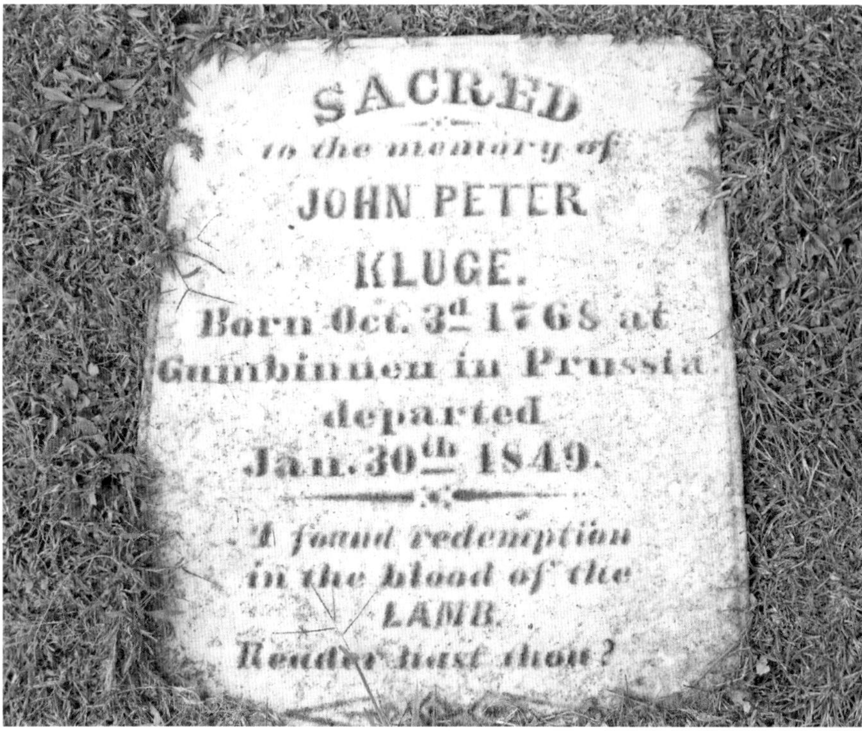

Grave marker of Moravian missionary John Kluge. *Courtesy of Leo Caldwell.*

tribes along with white traders. The missionaries had difficulties obtaining adequate supplies of goods, even with the trader activity. The missionaries also found a great deal of alcohol abuse among the Lenape. Overall, the diaries suggest a condescending attitude of the missionaries toward their neighbors and a general misunderstanding of what was happening to the Lenape. The Lenape's attitude at the time seems to be one of indifference toward the mission.

The mission never was able to pull in enough converts nor convince enough Lenape even to listen. The memory of the devastating massacre at Gnadenhütten left many indifferent or hostile to the Moravian church. Some believed that the Moravians wanted to convert them in order to render them "tame" or complacent against settler aggression. The missionaries in east-central Indiana even speak of a Lenape woman who was "constantly telling them that the Brethren merely wanted to make the Indians tame, so that the white people might kill them as had been done in Gnadenhütten."[322] Tribal leaders shared this attitude, with Buckhongehelas telling the missionaries that "we cannot drop our customs and teaching and sacrifices, for our forefathers too received them from God and left them to us. Every Indian must remain true to these things and not let them go. Your teaching is only for white people, and you yourselves see that we have another skin."[323] The missionaries failed "to develop a sympathetic understanding of Indian traits, and this failure was a contributory cause of the disaster which attended the mission."[324] Unless referring to a convert, the missionaries would almost always refer to their Lenape neighbors as heathens: "The Indians had a drunken carousal in the heathen town four miles from here,"[325] and, "Many heathen Indians rode through our place on their way to a sacrifice in Woapicamikunk."[326] As the years turned, it became clear to the missionaries that they were not wanted, as Kluge wrote in the diaries that "their desire is to attract to themselves as many Indians as they can, in order to make a strong outward appearance. For the word of God, they care nothing at all."[327] By the spring of 1806, deciding to remain in Indiana was a question of not just hospitality but also life and death.

Chapter 9

Witch Hunts

In the 1700s, we find numerous instances of Lenape cultural changes, both religious and political, in response to the external pressures as they moved inland. These changes were "the development of new cultural forms, in response to situational demands"[328] that were "adaptive innovations which do not result in any approximation of a foreign culture."[329] In a few instances, Lenape nativist movements arose "whose thesis was that the Indian's lot had been much happier before the arrival of the European, and would once again improve if, by some means or other, the Indian could again live without the white man."[330] In the mid-1700s, prophets appeared among the Lenape, which "developed along two divergent lines,"[331] with the Munsee prophet Papounhan preaching nonviolence coupled with a strict adherence to ancient customs. Another prophet named Neolin, whose nativist preaching encouraged a return to the old ways, may have influenced Pontiac in his rebellion.[332] Neolin's preaching spearheaded a "nativist revival"[333] that "helped lead to a new stirring of anti-European sentiment, a sort of "Indian nationalism" that was harnessed by Chief Pontiac.[334] Neolin's teaching also involved modification of sacred rites already in place, and this pushed the Lenape "toward practices reflective of aboriginal ones."[335] The "[m]emory of these practices survived among the Delawares for the next two centuries."[336] Another Munsee-speaking Lenape prophet named Wangomen followed in a similar vein as Neolin. Wangomen is unique in the fact that he requested from the Lupwaaeenóàuk in the 1770s to seek out witches and other Lenape engaged in sorcery in order to purge them from the tribe.[337]

While those movements fizzled out, they were in the collective memory of the White River Lenape in the early 1800s.

Buckhongahelas died on May 24, 1805, according to the Moravians, and his death "brought about a veritable revolution among the heathen, because…they do not believe that he died a natural death."[338] A particularly harsh winter in 1804–5 had made life difficult in the villages, and a series of floods ruined crops in 1805 and 1806. Disease also ravaged through the villages at this time, and this affected "people suddenly and kill[ed] them within days."[339] The situation soon grew out of hand, and long-standing "tensions that had grown along the White River for years began to boil over."[340] The Lenape laid blame on themselves for turning on the Creator, while others blamed "malignant spiritual power by evilly disposed persons."[341] Some even blamed the Moravians and their converts for the problems.[342]

In 1805 and 1806, a Munsee-speaking woman named Beata began having visions, compelling her to preach "a return to the old ways, which was endorsed by the Delaware chiefs."[343] Her visions included visitations from strange men who warned her that God was not happy with the Lenape and that if they did not live as they did along the Atlantic coast "a terrible storm will arise and break down all the trees in the woods, and all Indians shall lose their lives in it."[344] Later visions included a visitation from God, who gave her a white light to swallow in order to speak only his words.[345] Beata preached that not only should the rituals be renewed, but the tribe must also forgo "all evil, drinking, fornification, stealing, murder, and the like."[346] Beata's popularity grew, and she became revered among the Lenape. Her stature—following a long tradition from Papounhan to Neolin and Wangomen—allowed her to act "as a judge, pronouncing to the community all offenses, such as witchcraft, which had been committed in strictest secrecy."[347] The evils being experienced by the White River Lenape—the disease, the flooding and the loss of a great chief—were attributed to sorcery and witchcraft.

Then, in April 1805, Lalawethika, the heavyset, partially blind brother of Tecumseh, was living at his brother's camp downriver on the White. He "gasped, dropped [his pipe], and toppled over on his side."[348] His wife believed him to have died. The neighbors believed him to be in another drunken stupor, as he was prone to do.[349] Lalawethika arose two days later, surprising his wife and neighbors and recounting a vision where "the Master of Life sent two handsome young men to carry his soul into the spirit world."[350] Once there, Lalawethika was allowed to gaze on heaven and see its greatness. He warned that Shawnee who sinned would be "reduced to

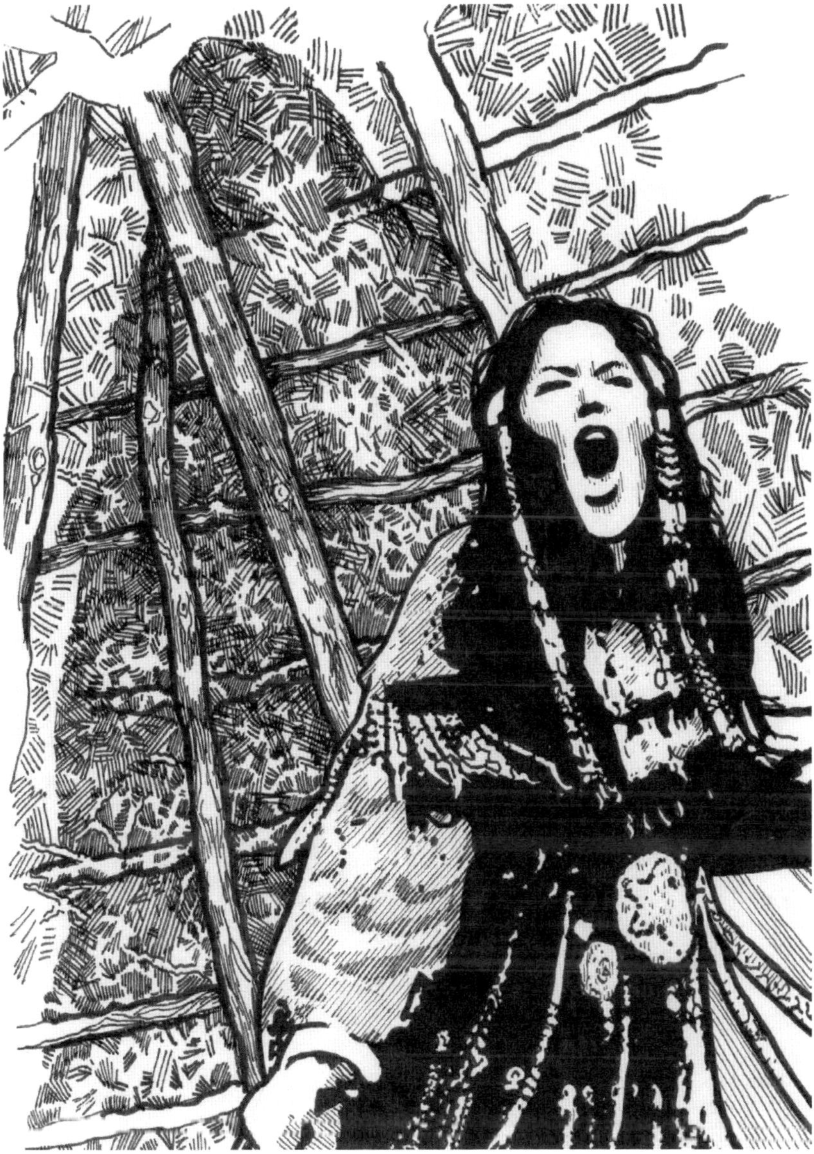

Beata's visions were significant to the White River Lenape. *Courtesy of George Everett Keller.*

ashes"[351] and that "unrepentant drunkards were forced to swallow molten lead until flames shot from their mouths."[352] After relating this vision, Lalawethika informed them that he was reborn as Tenskwatawa, meaning "open door," and began preaching as a Shawnee prophet.[353] While it is

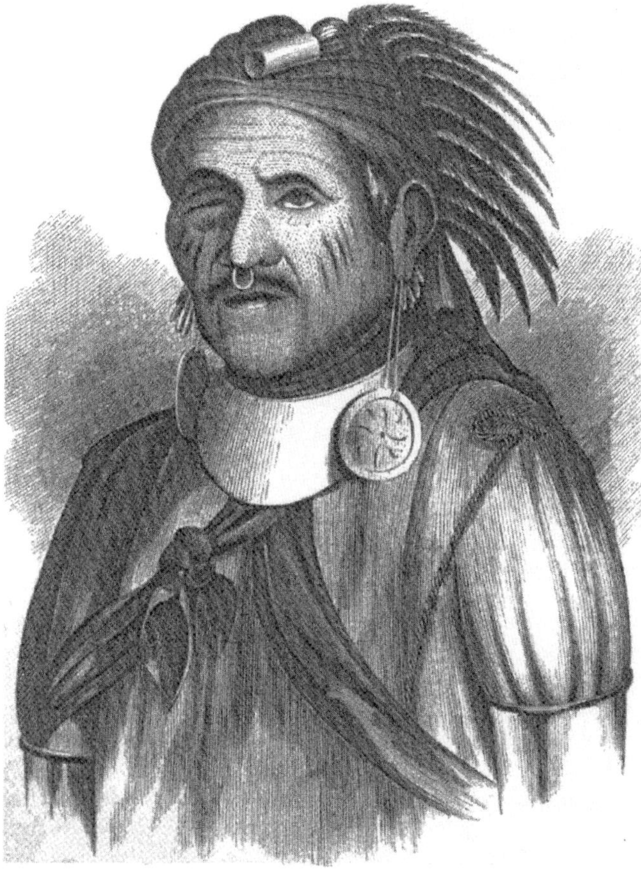

Engraving of the "Shawnee Prophet" Lalawethika (Tenskwatawa). *Wikicommons.*

unclear the exact connection between the Shawnee Prophet and Beata, the popularity of Beata's teachings and the calamities occurring on the White River at the time suggest a strong connection—or, as Tecumseh's biographer

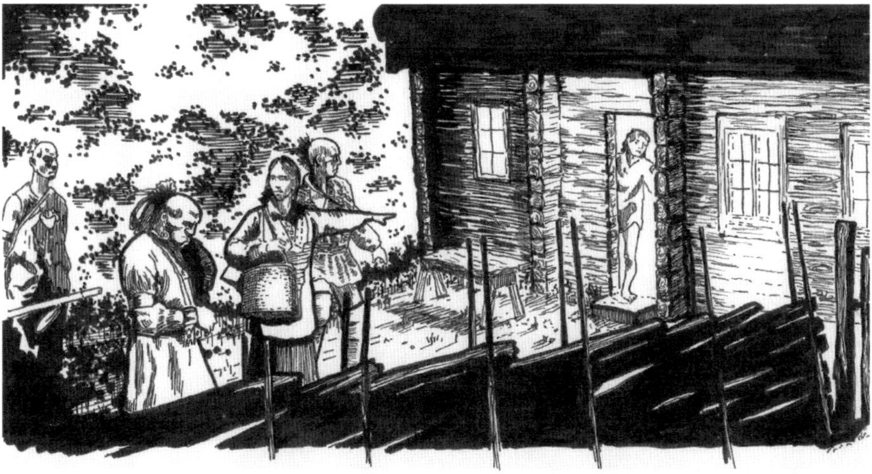

Sources indicate at least six deaths during the "witch hunts" on the White River. *Courtesy of George Everett Keller.*

Sugden suggested, "More than anyone else, the Delaware prophetess Beata promoted Lalawéthika's new career."[354]

Tenkswatawa was then invited by the followers of Beata to "root out witches en masse"[355] at a specially arranged council of judgment. Soon after, many Lenape from the villages began arriving for the special council at either Tetepachsit's, or Buckhongehelas's village. The council targeted Lenape who had become either too friendly with or too dependent on whites, Moravian converts and chiefs who were "discredited and charged with witchcraft,"[356] all of which "created a climate of fear, particularly among the old and individuals whose behavior was known to be antisocial."[357] This special council in March 1806, with Tenskwatawa as a prosecutor, identified the accused and "rounded up suspected witches and began to torture them to confess."[358] While the total number of people accused and executed in the witch hunts is unknown, the written records indicate a few by name.[359]

One of the first to have died was Anne Charity, or Caritas. An elderly woman, she was an "outspoken critic of Beata,"[360] a Moravian convert and steadfast Christian and was known for her fastidious cleanliness.[361] The story of her death suggests that she was killed by being slowly washed with fire. The researcher Jay Miller discovered that being washed with fire actually meant "she was probably scrubbed with water mixed with woodash and lye."[362]

Joshua, the Moravian's Mohican convert, was identified as a witch and burned alive at the stake in Tetepachsit's, or Buckhongehelas's village. Young Lenape men with their faces painted black led Joshua away for execution.

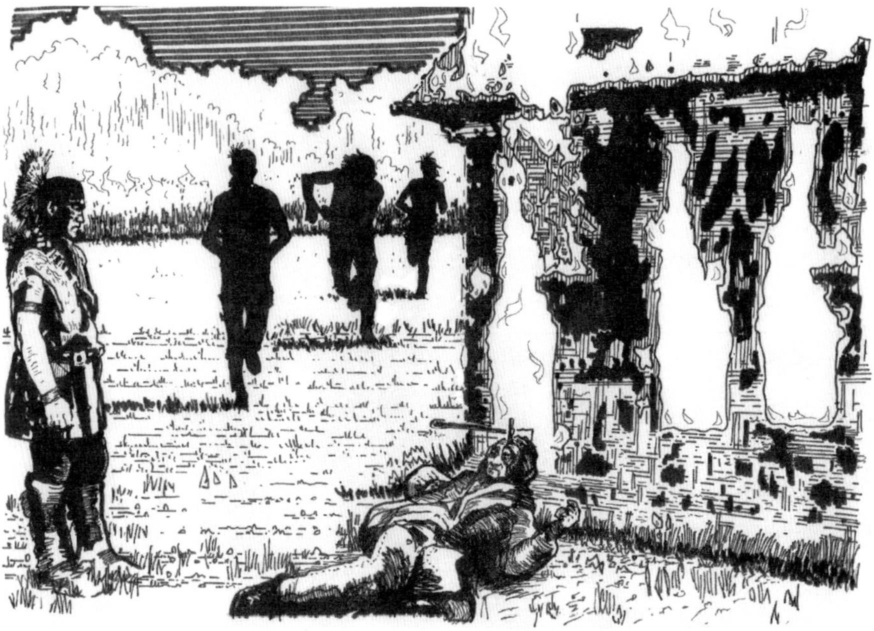

Tetepachsit being tomahawked and burned alive during the witch hunts in 1806. *Courtesy of George Everett Keller.*

Chief Tetepachsit was also marked as a witch, probably because he had signed away Lenape hunting ground in an earlier treaty or perhaps because he married a second wife, angering the son of his first. Tetepachsit was taken to the Moravian's mission and burned. In their diaries, the Moravians tell the story as follows on March 17, 1806:

> *We were overcome with terror and fright when all of a sudden we saw ten Indians with their faces painted black, some on foot, others on horseback, coming into our village with old Chief Tedpachsit. Soon after these barbarians built a large fire near our place, struck the old Chief on the head with the hatchet and threw him half-alive into the fire. Meanwhile they stood near and rejoiced over the pitiful cries and movements of the unfortunate one. The plain south of our village and the woods caught fire so that our village was full of smoke and fumes.*[363]

Tetepachsit's nephew, Billy Patterson, was also burned alive. Tetepachsit's wife and Chief Hockingpomsga narrowly avoided execution during the trials. It is possible that two Nanticoke women were burned during the trials and perhaps two other women a few years earlier under similar circumstances.[364] By late spring, the news of the executions had reached Governor William Henry Harrison. Alarmed, Harrison sent a letter begging them to stop: "Let your poor old men and women sleep in quietness, and banish from their minds the dreadful idea of being burnt alive by their own friends and countrymen."[365]

The consequences of the witch trials compelled the Moravians to leave and propelled Tenskwatawa's stature. After being warned by a French trader,[366] the Moravians requested from their elders to abandon the mission and head back east, which they did in the fall of 1806. Tenskwatawa began preaching across the Indiana territory and Ohio, converting many to his cause. Starting in Greenville, Ohio, Tenskwatawa lead his followers to "Prophetstown" near present-day Lafayette. Always a thorn in Governor Harrison's side, Tenskwatawa's village was attacked by Harrison on November 11 at the Battle of Tippecanoe. Tenskwatawa was defeated, and his stature waned. He continued operating under Tecumseh during the War of 1812. After the Shawnee and British defeat, Tenskwatawa lived in Canada for a while before moving with his tribe to Kansas. His legacy in Indiana is both tragic and fascinating. His involvement with the Lenape witch hunts should not be understated, "but we should be careful not to exaggerate his involvement.

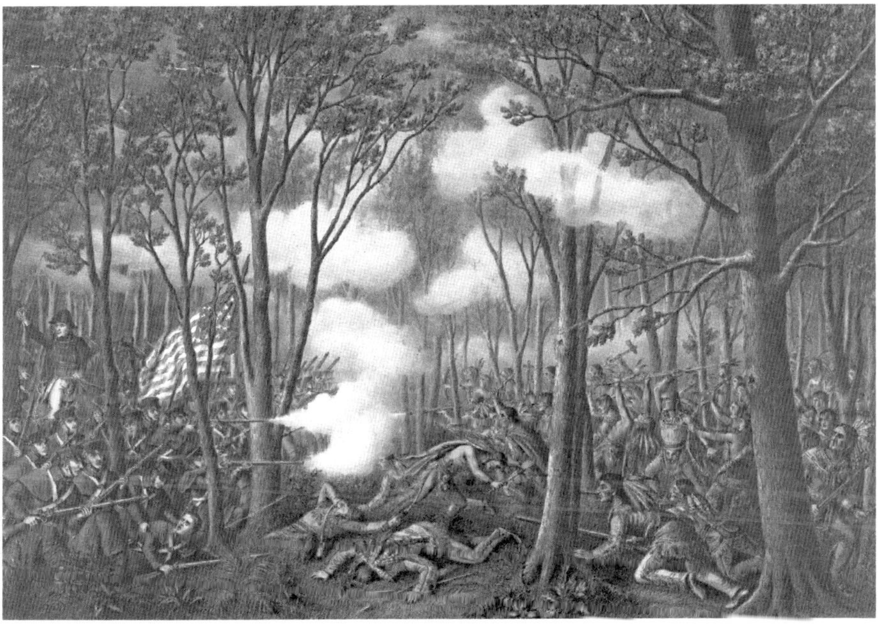

Engraving of the Battle of Tippecanoe. *Courtesy of the Library of Congress.*

The reform movement had begun long before Lalawéthika's intervention, and he was an expression, not a cause of it."[367]

For the Lenape, the reforms suggested by Beata modified a ceremonial rite referred to as the Gamwing or Big House Ceremony, which became fully initiated in 1812 or 1813.[368] The witch trials likely contributed to legends that were passed down as stories in both Lenape and white worlds.[369] Early settlers recount of "Indian torture stakes" on property near the site of Buckhonhehelas' Town, Tetepachsit's Town and in Yorktown.[370] These settlers may have been familiar with the events in 1806. What they see as torture stakes, described as long wooden poles with faces carved into them, were most likely not connected with the witch trials at all and were the support posts for the ceremonial Gamwing structure.

Chapter 10

The Big House Ceremony

By the time the Lenape had moved west of the Mississippi River, they were conducting a special annual ceremony known as Gamwing, or the Big House Ceremony. While scholars disagree on the exact evolution of the rite, "the majority of scholars who have done fieldwork among Delawares agree that the Gamwing was an ancient expression of Delaware traditions, albeit modified over time."[371] Gamwing was the Lenape "integrative rite, expressing community identity and cosmic harmony from ancient times."[372] As the decentralized Unami and Munsee speakers moved west from their ancestral homelands, the rite was modified, providing a ritual in which the entire community could celebrate together.

The rite lasted twelve days in which "families worshiped in a special building symbolic of the universe, renewing their spiritual ties with all of creation."[373] By the time it was celebrated in Oklahoma, the Big House Ceremony took place in fall and was sponsored annually by one of the three phratries. Specialized dances and vision songs became crucial components of the ceremony.[374] The Big House itself was built of logs, with a wooden shingle roof and "doors at both the east and west ends of the building,"[375] and "large carvings of [a] face were the only decorative features of the ceremonial building."[376] The carved faces on a center post, painted half black and half red, symbolized the Misi'ng, a spirit that appeared to the Lenape informing them to revive the ceremony after a brief cessation of its celebration.[377] The vestiges of this post with the carved Misi'ng are probably what the early settlers found along the White River in the early-middle

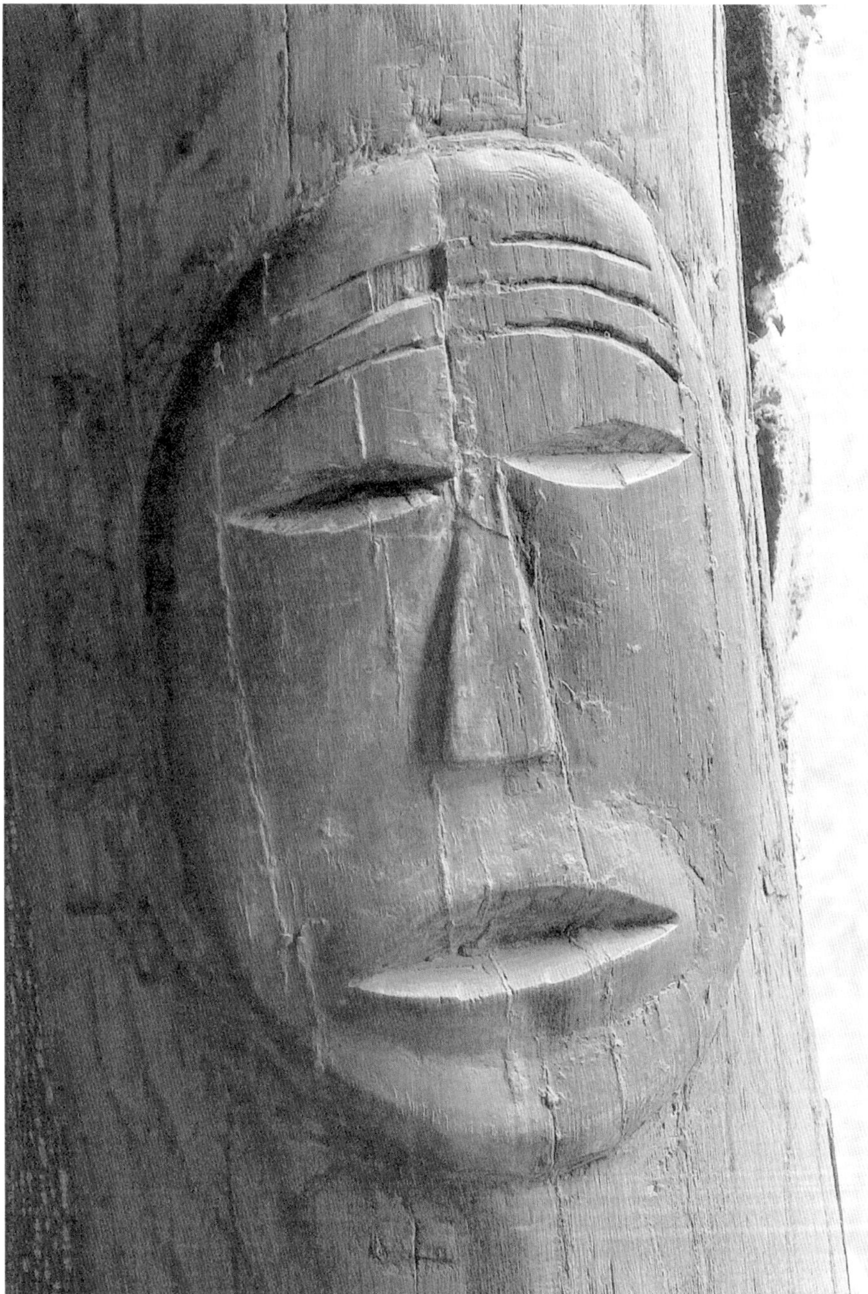

M'Sing wood carving, similar to carvings in the Big House. *Courtesy of State Museum of Pennsylvania, Historical and Museum Commission.*

1800s in Indiana. The Big House building had two ceremonial fires on the inside near the center post, and a masked dancer, wearing a suit made of tanned bearskin with the hair still attached, played a crucial part. During the ceremony, it was common for participants to have visions and relate their insights to fellow Lenape.[378]

The exact origins of the ceremony are unknown, but likely it was an evolution of the Thanksgiving Rite, which had been celebrated among the Lenape before European contact. However, as the Lenape moved west, the ritual was modified, with the last major change to the ceremony coming from Beata.[379] Beata moved the rite from spring to fall and also gave women a more significant role in the ceremony.[380] Another Lenape festival, known as the Green Corn Rite, was celebrated among many Algonquian-speaking groups in the Eastern Woodlands in late summer. However, as Beata's reforms modified the spring Thanksgiving Rite to the fall Big House Ceremony, the Green Corn Rite gave way to the new celebration, ending in 1867.[381] The Big House Ceremony was practiced by Oklahoma Lenape until 1924 and was briefly revived during World War II.

Lenape legend has the origins of the Big House Ceremony commencing after an earthquake, when "many long years ago the Delawares quit their church completely. After a bit, an earthquake started. The earth trembled and shook for days. Finally, a spirit appeared to the people telling them to return to the Big House or else."[382] Other legends speak of a "time when the earth quaked, so it is said, a great crackling, rumbling noise arose here from down in the ground below. And there came rising dust and smoke, while here and there came rising something sticky, looking like tar, a black fluid."[383] As the legend goes, the event was a warning to return to the Big House. The anthropologist Jay Miller understood the legend to suggest that the Big House Ceremony was revived after the massive New Madrid earthquakes in 1811–12, where "the rite was waning by the end of the [1800–1810] decade, only to be revived by massive earthquakes in the central Mississippi valley."[384] Centered on the New Madrid Seismic Zone, four massive earthquakes happened between December 1811 and February 1812, each probably registering over 8.0 on the Richter Scale. Stories from the time indicate that the Mississippi River ran backward, river banks collapsed, whole villages were destroyed and uncommon geological occurrences terrified white, Native and black populations in the Mississippi and Ohio River Valleys.[385] The earthquakes and their aftershocks "had a profound effect on Natives,"[386] and perhaps this was the source of the Big House Ceremony legend. The legends speak of "something sticky, looking like tar, a black fluid"[387] appearing on the surface. It is not uncommon for small amounts of underground oil to appear on the surface as "tar balls" or for oil to ooze in certain spots, known as an oil seep. While this is entirely speculative, the Trenton Oil and Gas Field sits beneath most of east-central Indiana and at one time had at least 1 billion barrels of oil.

Chapter 11

The War of 1812

After the Moravians left, the dearth of firsthand written documents leaves some mystery about the lives of the White River Lenape. We do know that the Treaty of Fort Wayne was signed on September 17, 1809, ceding land in the Whitewater River Valley to the Indiana territorial government. White River Lenape, Miami, Shawnee, Kickapoo and the Potawatomi all signed the treaty.[388] John Conner served as interpreter for the Lenape.[389] The treaty is interesting as it indicates Miami recognition of Lenape landownership, with Article 2 stating, "The Miamies explicitly acknowledge the equal right of the Delawares with themselves to the country watered by the White River."[390] The treaty was signed by Captain Killbuck, Amochk (the Beaver), Petchekekapon and Kikthawenund. Kikthawenund had Hockingpomsga's proxy apparently, as the former made the mark for the latter, who was not present at the treaty signing, indicating that he was still alive in 1809.

As Tecumseh and Tenskwatawa (Lalawethika) gained followers, the Lupwaaeenóáuk "had voted not to support Tecumseh, and there were no Delawares sanctioned by the Council with the Prophet's forces at Tippecanoe, although there may have been a few impulsive young warriors looking for excitement."[391] The Lenape voted to stay out of this war and remain neutral. While we do not know the specifics of the decision, it is likely that John and William Conner's influence assisted in the neutral stance.[392] The tribe did at one point attempt to intervene and persuade Tenskwatawa to give up his fight. As Harrison's army marched north from Vincennes to Prophetstown in the fall of 1811, a group of Lenape chiefs with John Conner "visited the

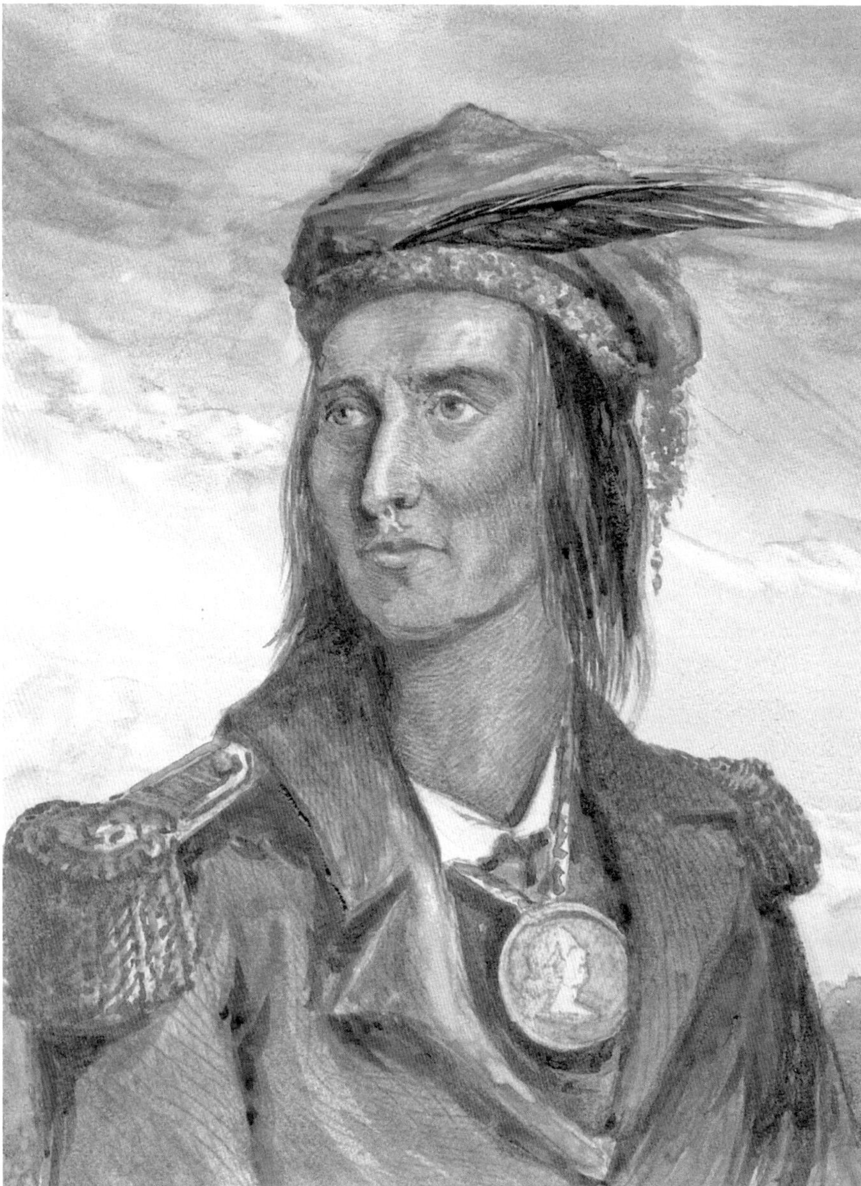

Portrait of Tecumseh. *Courtesy of Internet Archive.*

prophet, and endeavored to dissuade him from adopting measures of active hostility against the people of the United States."[393] Tenskwatawa sent the Lenape on their way, telling them that they could do as they pleased, but "declared that his tomahawk was up against the whites"[394] and that he "was boasting of burning the first American prisoner he took."[395] Tenskwatawa's forces were defeated in early November 1811 and again in the fall of 1812, shattering his religious movement. Tecumseh was in the Southeast attempting to bring new tribes into his alliance. He returned in the late winter of 1812 and began "immediately to rebuild the faltering confederacy."[396] The massive New Madrid earthquakes in late 1811 and early 1812 increased Tecumseh's followers.[397] Tecumseh's force eventually aligned with the British during the War of 1812, but he had a difficult time bringing all of Indiana's tribes into his confederacy.

By early 1812, general turmoil reigned in Indiana. Reports of indigenous attacks on settler camps and white reprisals exist throughout early 1812. Many of tribal leaders in Indiana felt that Tenskwatawa was to blame. In May of that year, Tecumseh organized a grand council of tribal leaders on the Mississinewa River near Peru—Shawnee, Miami, Kickapoo, Lenape, Piankashaw, Wyandot, Wea, Winnebago, Ottawa and Ojibwe were in attendance.[398] Tecumseh's hope was that these leaders would bring their tribes into his confederacy. At the council, the Potawatomi pointed out that Tecumseh's brother Tenskwatawa was an imposter and that his teachings caused some hotheads to kill white settlers. Tecumseh attempted a reply about the proper understanding of Shawnee counsel but was cut off by a Lenape captain:

> *We have not met at this place to listen to such words. The red people have been killing the whites. The just resentment of the latter is raised against the former. Our white brethren are on their feet—their guns in their hands. There is no time for us to tell each other, You have done this, and you have done that. If there was, we could tell the prophet that both red and white people have felt the bad effects of his counsel. Let us all join our hearts and hands together, and proclaim peace through the land of the red people. Let us make our voices be heard and respected, and rely on the justice of our white brethren.*[399]

By the outbreak of the War of 1812, both "the Miamis and the Delawares continued to make declarations of their friendship for the United States; but that they expressed a wish to preserve a state of neutrality during the war."[400] True to form, not all Lenape followed their chief's directives. In September 1812, a small party of Shawnee and perhaps Lenape raided the pioneer settlement of Pigeon Roost near Scottsburg, Indiana. The raiding party killed "one man, five woman, and sixteen children."[101] The raid was part of a larger effort by Tecumseh to attack white settlements in retaliation for the defeat at Tippecanoe.[102] Fort Wayne and Fort Harrison were also attacked in the same year. A militia of settlers followed the raiders north with an attempt to attack White River Lenape villages, "some of whom were suspected of having been engaged in the destruction of the Pigeon Roost settlement."[103] However, the militia did not make it far, attacking some of the raiders near the Muscatatuck River, while the rest got away.

After the Potawatomi assault on Fort Wayne in September 1812, Harrison decided to attack all Native villages in the area, starting with the Miami. While it is likely that Miami warriors did fight with the Potawatomi, the main body remained neutral. The recent death of Chief Little Turtle meant that finding a mitigating force to negotiate the difficult situation on the side of the Miami was lost for Harrison. The Americans attempted a peace negotiation at Piqua, Ohio, but the Miami did not attend. John Conner informed Governor Harrison that "the Miami were urging the Delawares to join them in a war against the United States."[104] Harrison ordered John Campbell, a lieutenant colonel in the United States Army, to lead a force of Kentucky dragoons against the villages along the Mississinewa River. Harrison gave Campbell explicit instructions to not harm the Lenape on the White. Harrison felt that any violence toward them "would be unfortunate, as the faith of the government has been pledged for their safety."[105] Harrison requested that William Conner move the main body of White River Lenape to Piqua during the war for safety and to generally keep them out of the war altogether.[106]

Once Conner returned from the task, he served as a guide for Campbell's expedition to the Mississinewa.[107] On December 17, 1812, Campbell's force attacked a Miami village on the Mississinewa near present-day Jalapa. It was "inhabited by a number of Delawares and Miamis. The troops rushed into the town, killed eight warriors, and took forty-two prisoners, eight of whom are warriors; the residue are women and children."[108] Campbell's force burned the village and a few others in the vicinity. The next day, the force assaulted the village again, this time meeting fierce indigenous resistance. Campbell's force won the day, but not before eight of his men died, with forty-two wounded. At least fifteen warriors were killed, but probably more. Most of the prisoners were Munsee-speaking Lenape, along with a few of those killed in battle.[109] Before marching back, Campbell sent a message to the remaining Lenape on the White River informing them to move to Piqua with their brethren. He also apologized for killing several Munsee, assuring them that "their people, in his power, would be compensated, by the government, for their losses."[110] The American forces simply did not want the Lenape to enter the war on the side of Tecumseh and the British.

In June 1813, an American colonel named Joseph Bartholomew led a force against the supposedly abandoned White River Lenape villages "with the intention to surprise and punish some hostile Indians who were supposed to be lurking about those villages."[111] Bartholomew not only found the villages empty but also that someone had burned most of them before his arrival, after the Lenape left for Piqua. He did find stores of corn, which he burned under the impression "that the hostile Indians were making use of it." The following month, Colonel William Russell led a much larger force through the same area, with an intention of neutralizing Native opposition along the Mississinewa.[112] He, too, found the Lenape towns abandoned. Throughout the war, the main body remained at Piqua, with unsanctioned warriors fighting with Tecumseh and another force fighting with William Conner on the side of the Americans.[113] Many of the Lenape had moved back to the White River by 1814 and had signed another Treaty of Greenville on July 22, 1814, which stated that they would give "their aid to the United States in prosecuting the war against Great-Britain, and such of the Native American tribes as still continue hostile; and to make no peace with either without the consent of the United States."[114] The Lenape chiefs that signed the treaty included Kikthawenund, James Nanticoke, Lapponnichle, Johnny Cake, Killbuck, Captain Buck, Captain White Eyes, Captain Pipe (Tahunqueecoppi) and several others.

Chapter 12

Final Years

At the end of the war, it became clear to all tribes in Indiana to move west. With the defeat of the British and Tecumseh went any hope of organized resistance in the Old Northwest territories. Indiana was opened to white settlement, and pioneers began pouring over the borders from Ohio, Kentucky, Illinois and Michigan—the White River Lenape found themselves trapped in the middle. The Indiana territorial government "found itself under strong public pressure to remove the Indians and make way for white settlements."[115] As Indiana became a state in 1816, officials took the policy of making peace with the tribes, legally obtaining their land and moving them west of the Mississippi. Both state and federal officials employed tactics involving "threats, cajolery, bribes, and all manner of intimidation, even though the Indians were paid for the territory they vacated."[116] For the Lenape and many other tribes, this resulted in the signing of the Treaty of St. Mary's in 1818 at St. Mary's, Ohio. Referred to as the "New Purchase," eight tribes—including the Wyandot, Seneca, Shawnee, Ottawa, Potawatomi, Wea, Miami and Lenape—signed six treaties, ceding most of their land in Indiana.[117] The treaty specific to the Lenape "resulted in the wholesale removal of the Delawares from Indiana,"[118] giving the tribe three years to vacate. The treaty provided land for the Lenape west of the Mississippi River in present-day Missouri, cash, a blacksmith and land reservations for Brotherton Native Americans, referred to as "York Indians," living near present-day Yorktown. In the Miami treaty at St. Mary's, the granddaughter of Chief Little Turtle was provided a land reservation at the site of the

Munsee Village, or what was once called Tetepachsit's Town. No fewer than eighteen Lenape chiefs signed the treaty, with Chief Kikthawenund being the primary leader at the time of the treaty's signing.

Brotherton in East-Central Indiana

Just prior to the signing of the Treaty of St. Mary's, Kikthawenund had invited a group of Lenape allies still living near ancestral lands to move to the White River.[119] This group consisted of Stockbridge Mahicans and later Brotherton, or Brothertown Pequot and Mohegan groups. The Stockbridge and Brotherton had strong cultural, matrimonial and lingual affiliation with Lenape speakers still living in New York. As the Lenape signed the Treaty of St. Mary's, the promised space for the invited Stockbridge and Brotherton vanished. As the main body of Stockbridge and Brotherton began their journey to Indiana, they learned that they had no land to move to. Many ultimately removed to Wisconsin, where they remain today.[120] However, several land reservations were made for the Brotherton families who had already moved ahead of the group, having arrived before 1818. They were living at the "York Indian Village" on a bluff overlooking the confluence of Buck Creek and the White River in present-day Yorktown.[121] The Brotherton were known to early white settlers as "York Indians," and after platting the first white settlement near the spot, Oliver Smith named the town "Yorktown" in recognition.[122] In the Treaty of St. Mary's, several Brothertons are listed as receiving land reservations, including Isaac Wobby, Samuel Cassman, Elizabeth Petchaka, Jacob Dick, Solomon Tindell and Benoni Tindell.[123] The treaty refers to them as "all of whom are Delawares," but this is unlikely with the exception of Cassman, whose identity is unknown.[124]

McCoy and Trowbridge

The Lenape had three years to organize their move west. We know a little about what went on during this time. The Baptist minister Isaac McCoy visited both Kikthawenund and William Conner a few times in 1818 and 1819. McCoy found Kikthawenund to be quite cordial when he arrived at Anderson's Town in December 1818, remarking, "He was very hospitable, prepared food for us, and endeavored to make us comfortable."[125] On a later trip to Vincennes, McCoy happened across Billy Killbuck, who was imprisoned for killing two white men while intoxicated,[126] further giving evidence to the continual abuse of alcohol by some and the illegal sale of it by white settlers. In May 1819, McCoy returned to Kikthawenund's village, finding him less convivial.[127] The chief seemed generally annoyed by McCoy's and related stories of whites killing Lenape.[128] By the time McCoy had left the White River, he could converse in Unami, having received lessons from a man named Ben Gray.[129]

Charles Trowbridge also visited the White River in the years following the Lenape's move west to interview remaining tribal members. In 1823, he arrived in Indiana "on assignment from Governor Lewis Cass of Michigan"[130] tasked with learning "what he could of Delaware customs and the Delaware language."[131] Although the main body had left in 1821, Trowbridge spent time with William Conner and Captain Pipe (Tahunqueecoppi), resulting in hundreds of pages detailing the Unami language.[132]

The Move West

In the late summer of 1821, almost all of the White River Lenape gathered in the meadow below William Conner's home preparing to move to Missouri.[133] Conner's wife, Mekinges, "would leave for the West with the Delawares, in obedience to the tribal law that the Indian wife must stay with her people."[134] The assembled group probably included Kikthawenund, Mekinges and William Conner's six children, John Conner's wife and their children and about "two thousand other persons in the main body."[135] By this time, Kikthawenund "felt bitterly about the St. Mary's treaties which had deprived them of the lands on which the Delawares had lived since about 1795."[136] The tribe gathered in a battered state that summer, having suffered more than two decades from the ravages of warfare, disease, rampant alcoholism and mistreatment.[137] Later that year, "1,346 Delawares from Indiana and their 1,499 horses were taken across the Mississippi River via the boat ferry at Kaskaskia, Illinois, by Pierre Menard."[138] Another seven hundred or so were left behind at Vincennes for the winter due to disease and were starving.[139] Eventually, they "converged by prearrangement on the James River…in Missouri."[140] The life in Missouri was not pleasant, as the land was generally poor and the Lenape were engaged in territorial disputes with the Osage. Kikthawenund also requested financial compensation from the Miami for supposed murders that members of that tribe had committed during their time in Indiana.[111] After balking at first, the Miami agreed to a sum, which was rejected by Kikthawenund. Ultimately, United States government officials stepped in and resolved the conflict.[112] By 1830, Kikthawenund had moved his tribe again to Kansas, where the land was more hospitable. After moving the main body, the chief died in 1831.[113] After the American Civil War, the Lenape moved again to Cherokee territory in what is now northeast Oklahoma in Bartlesville. They remain here today as the Delaware Tribe of Indians.

THE REMAINING LENAPE AND GOLDSMITH GILBERT

Despite local legends to the contrary, there is no evidence to suggest that large numbers of Lenape remained in east-central Indiana after the tribe moved west. Written evidence suggests that a few remained behind, including Captain Pipe (Tahunqueecoppi) and James Musco. Often referred to in early sources as "Indian Jim," Musco remained behind with his parents, Jacob and Sally. The tradition as told by early settlers holds that "Jake Musco had had a definite falling out with his clan prior to the Delaware exodus, a murder or some such act of violence having apparently separated him from his tribe."[114] James lived for a time with Lewis Rees, having contributed to the construction of Delaware County's first schoolhouse.[115] He is buried in Rees Cemetery in southeast Delaware County. He died in 1873 at the approximate age of sixty-nine.

Not long after the Lenape, seven white settlers murdered a small hunting party of Native Americans near present-day Pendleton in an event known as the Fall Creek Massacre. The settlers came upon three families of Seneca on March 22, 1824. They proceeded to kill the three men, their wives and four children. The men were arrested and tried for murder, a remarkable event given the anti–Native American sentiment in Indiana at the time, although the legal proceedings may have been motivated by fear where "everyone in central Indiana feared retaliation from the Indians."[116] Most of the murderers were hanged after jurors found them guilty.

While the Fall Creek Massacre was probably the most extreme example of indigenous mistreatment at the hands of whites in Indiana, other settlers swindled reservation land from Native Americans. Often identified as the founder of Muncie, a white trader named Goldsmith Gilbert had a trading post at the Mississinewa River in 1823. The post was burned by a Miami or Lenape intoxicated on the whiskey that Gilbert probably had sold him.[147] Gilbert was awarded money by the government, which he used to purchase reservations awarded to Miami and Brotherton in the Treaty of St. Mary's. Gilbert started by purchasing the "Hackley Reserve" from Rebecca Hackley, 672 acres of land just north of the bend in the White River at the site of Munsee Town. Hackley was the granddaughter of Miami chief Little Turtle and the daughter of William Wells and Wanagapeth. Gilbert used his proceeds to purchase the tract for $960.[148] However, it appears that Gilbert failed to pay Hackley in a timely manner, as a suit was filed in 1841 for compensation, suggesting that "the transfer of land from Mrs. Hackley to Mr. Gilbert took many years and final resort to law before it was completed."[149]

Gilbert built commercial buildings just south of the Hackley Reserve and turned his attention to purchasing land held by Brotherton. Isaac Wobby, Samuel Cassman, Elizabeth Petchaka, Jacob Dick, Solomon Tindell and Benoni Tindell all received land in the Treaty of St. Mary's. The families of Wobby, Dick and Tindell all sold to Gilbert in the late 1820s or early 1830s.[150] Petchaka sold her land to a man named Jean Baptiste Valle in 1831.[151] Samuel Cassman "sold his granted land to Goldsmith Gilbert in 1836 after a five-year struggle regarding valuation."[152] Gilbert turned around and sold the land to Oliver Smith, who platted "Yorktown" on the site of the York Village. Cassman stood his ground and "with his sons had been victorious in a skirmish on Buck Creek where the quill in the hands of the scarcely literate was proved to be mightier than the arrow had been to win the Indian his rights in Indiana."[153] Cassman may have been Lenape or Brotherton—his exact origins are unknown. Legend has it that he was discovered dead inside a tree in Madison County in the 1840s, having attempted to take shelter there following a hunting trip in winter.[154]

Epilogue

It would take tens of thousands of pages to comprehensively explore the archaeological record and historical documents pertaining to Native Americans in east-central Indiana. As we saw in the introduction, pre-European contact human habitation along the west fork of the White River extends back about ten thousand years. Archaeologists discover new evidence, and historians revise and improve their understanding of post-contact tribes with renewed analysis of documents. While scholars continue to modify our collective knowledge, far too often this information does not translate into public knowledge. The lack of appropriate educational objectives, cultural myopia and disinterest in local history all contribute to ignorance of the indigenous cultures in east-central Indiana.

Despite these public knowledge defects, it is my hope that this book will instill in Hoosiers a deep interest in and respect for Native American history, culture, archaeology and understanding in Indiana. During my research, several archaeologists stressed the lack of synthesis in the local archaeological record, while also suggesting that a great deal of information is probably beneath the ground still just waiting to be discovered, analyzed and interpreted. Historians were quick to relate that the Lenape period in east-central Indiana was significant for the development of the state, yet far too often, Native contributions get pushed to the background with the scenery in historical narratives. If the general public can share scholarly interest, east-central Indiana might become an ideal place for new investigations into a relatively unknown past.

For those readers interested in learning more about the Adena, Ohio Hopewell, New Castle Phase, Oliver, Oneota, Western-Basin, Castor, Fort Ancient, Mississippian, Miami, Shawnee and Lenape cultures, look through the extensive bibliography of this book. Readers will find a variety of scholarly publications, books and archaeological reports. For those in the area, I encourage you to visit the Strawtown Koteewi Park in Strawtown, Mounds State Park in Anderson, the Eiteljorg Museum of American Indians and Western Art in Indianapolis and the Conner Prairie Interactive Museum in Fishers. Each location offers a rich assortment of artifacts and information pertaining to Native American culture, art, history and archaeology.

Notes

Introduction

1. The statues were placed in Muncie by members of the Ball family, *Appeal to the Great Spirit* by the family members of Edmund B. Ball and *Passing of the Buffalo* by the Petty family as homage to Fred Petty. The statues were made by the sculptor Cyrus Dallin and are of Sioux, or Ute, peoples and reflect idyllic features.
2. Haimbaugh, *History of Delaware County*, 43–84.
3. McCord and Cochran's list of radiocarbon dates in their chapter "Adena Complex" in *Transitions*, 348–49. The authors list the approximate date range for the mounds, enclosures and embankments in east-central Indiana. The earliest dates are as follows: Fiddleback Ditch (410 CE) and the New Castle Mound 4 (360 BCE).
4. Madison, *Hoosiers*, 2–74.
5. Peckham, *Indiana*.
6. Indiana Department of Education, *Indiana Academic Standards*, adopted in 2013.
7. Galloway, *Hernando de Soto Expedition*.
8. The terms derive from Willey and Phillips, *Method and Theory in American Archaeology*.
9. Silverberg, *Mound Builders*.
10. The New Castle Phase was first developed by Vickery in 1969. See Vickery, "'Reluctant' or 'Avant-Garde' Hopewell?"
11. Ibid.
12. Pauketat, *Cahokia*.

13. See Weslager, *Delaware Indians.*
14. Referencing Ives Goddard, Brice Obermeyer succinctly explained, "The Delaware Tribe is one of many contemporary tribes that descend from the Unami- and Munsee-speaking peoples of the Delaware and Hudson River valleys. Munsee and Unami are two closely related Algonquian dialects that were easily distinguishable from the languages of the other coastal Algonquian groups." Quote from Obermeyer, "Removal and the Cherokee-Delaware Agreement," 37–48, 52–58.
15. Woodward and McDonald, *Indian Mounds of the Middle Ohio Valley*, 7.
16. Mithen, *After the Ice.*
17. Ehlers and Gibbard, *Quaternary Glaciations.*
18. Mithen, *After the Ice.*
19. Stanford and Bradley, *Across Atlantic Ice*; Fagundes, Kanitz, Eckert, Valls et al., "Mitochondrial Population Genomics."
20. See Huckell and Kilby, *Clovis Caches.*
21. Tankersley, Smith and Cochran, "Early Paleoindian Land Use," 301–19.
22. Stanford and Bradley, *Across Atlantic Ice.*
23. Woodward and McDonald, *Indian Mounds of the Middle Ohio Valley.*
24. Ibid., 21.
25. Traits considered from the Woodland Period in this paragraph are referenced from Caldwell, *Trend and Tradition.*
26. McCullough, "Cultural Interaction Along the West Fork," 141–54.
27. Ibid., 154.
28. Items in this paragraph are referenced from Pauketat, *Cahokia.*
29. See Connolly and Lepper, *Fort Ancient Earthworks.*
30. Milner, *Moundbuilders*, 79–80.
31. Herrmann, Monaghan, Romain, Schilling et al., "New Multistage Construction Chronology."
32. Silverberg, *Mound Builders*, 29–49.
33. Ibid.
34. Witthoft and Hunter, "Seventeenth-Century Origins of the Shawnee," 42–57.
35. Emerson and Lewis, *Cahokia and the Hinterlands.*
36. Mann, *1491*; Mann, *1493.*

CHAPTER 1

37. Cochran, "Culture History of Indiana."
38. Ibid. Cochran has that "the hallmark of Paleoindian technology is the fluted spear point. Fluted points are reported from most counties in Indiana although they occur in low densities."

39. Woodward and McDonald, *Indian Mounds of the Middle Ohio Valley*, 10–11.
40. Smith and Yarnell, "Initial Formation of an Indigenous Crop Complex," 6,561–66.
41. Diamond and Ordunio, *Guns, Germs and Steel*, 126.
42. Emerson, McElrath and Fortier, *Late Woodland Societies*, 3–36.
43. Ibid., 16.
44. Nolan and Howard, "Using Evolutionary Archaeology," 145.
45. McCord and Cochran, "Adena Complex."
46. Ibid., 356–57.
47. Fagan, *First North Americans*, 203.
48. Fagan, "Adena Culture," *Oxford Companion to Archaeology*, 1.
49. Ibid.
50. Clay, "Essential Features of Adena Ritual," 2.
51. Kellar, *Introduction to the Prehistory of Indiana*, 37.
52. Fagan, *First North Americans*, 203.
53. Hays, "Adena Mortuary Patterns in Central Ohio," 106–20.
54. Ibid., 203–8. Quote from 204.
55. Silverberg, *Mound Builders*, 186–87.
56. Clay, "Essential Features of Adena Ritual," 9.
57. Ibid.
58. Silverberg, *Mound Builders*, 184–85.
59. Ibid.
60. Abrams, "Hopewell Archaeology," 172.
61. Ibid.
62. Woodward and McDonald, *Indian Mounds of the Middle Ohio Valley*, 23.
63. Ibid.
64. Fagan, *First North Americans*, 210.
65. Dancey, *Ohio Hopewell Community Organization*.
66. Ibid.
67. Ibid., 3.
68. Woodward and McDonald, *Indian Mounds of the Middle Ohio Valley*, 46–47.
69. Fagan, *First North Americans*, 214.
70. Ibid.
71. Woodward and McDonald, *Indian Mounds of the Middle Ohio Valley*, 51.

CHAPTER 2

72. Quote was taken directly from McCord and Cochran, *Fudge Site*, 105–6. See also Ball State University's Applied Anthropology Laboratory at http://cms.bsu.edu/academics/centersandinstitutes/applied-anthropology-laboratories/publications.

73. Kent Vickery originally proposed the name New Castle Phase to "accommodate two related earthwork complexes in east-central Indiana: the Anderson Group…in Mounds State Park, Madison County, and the New Castle Complex…in nearby Henry County. Temporally, these sites fall within the Middle Woodland period; culturally, they are apparently transitional between Adena and Hopewell." Quote taken from Vickery, "'Reluctant' or 'Avant-Garde' Hopewell?"
74. All information in this paragraph is from McCord and Cochran, *Fudge Site*, unless otherwise cited.
75. McCord and Cochran's list of radiocarbon dates in their chapter "Adena Complex," 337.
76. Ibid.
77. McCord and Cochran, *Fudge Site*, 107.
78. Ibid.
79. Ibid., 108.
80. Ibid.
81. The list is derived from McCord and Cochran, *Fudge Site*, 108.
82. Ibid.
83. Ibid., 109.
84. Ibid.
85. Cochran and McCord, "Archaeology of Anderson Mounds," 6.
86. Ibid., 8.
87. Woodward and McDonald, *Indian Mounds of the Middle Ohio Valley*, 103.
88. Cochran and McCord, "Archaeology of Anderson Mounds," 8.
89. Ibid., 9.
90. Woodward and McDonald, *Indian Mounds of the Middle Ohio Valley*, 105.
91. Ibid.
92. Ibid., 105–6.
93. Ibid., 106.
94. McCord and Cochran, *Fudge Site*, 1.
95. Ibid.
96. Ibid., 86.
97. Ibid.
98. Ibid., 96.
99. McCord, "New Castle Site Revisited," 16–18.
100. Ibid., 18–28.
101. Ibid.

CHAPTER 3

102. McCord and Cochran, "Woodland Sites in East Central Indiana," 161.
103. Woodward and McDonald, *Indian Mounds of the Middle Ohio Valley*, 69.
104. Ibid., 69.
105. McCord and Cochran, "Woodland Sites in East Central Indiana," 161.
106. Ibid.
107. Ibid., 166.
108. Ibid.
109. Cochran, "Culture History of Indiana."
110. Graham and McCullough, "Archaeological Investigation of Two Western Basin Tradition-Related Sites," 27.
111. McCord and Cochran, "Archaeological Survey of the Taylor Property," 32.
112. Willey and Phillips, *Method and Theory in American Archaeology*, 167.
113. Indiana Department of Natural Resources, *Indiana Archaeology*, 67.
114. Ibid., 64.
115. Ibid., 31.
116. Ibid., 81.
117. Graham and McCullough, "Archaeological Investigation of Two Western Basin Tradition-Related Sites," 171.
118. Woodward and McDonald, *Indian Mounds of the Middle Ohio Valley*, 70.
119. Kellar, *Introduction to the Prehistory of Indiana*, 52.
120. Ibid.
121. Ibid., 61.
122. Ibid., 61–62.

CHAPTER 4

123. Dillon, *History of Indiana*, 2–3.
124. Esarey, *History of Indiana*, 9.
125. Ibid.
126. Ibid., 14.
127. Ibid., 20–22.
128. Ibid.; Dillon, *History of Indiana*.
129. Cayton, *Frontier Indiana*, 54.
130. Ibid., 53.
131. Rafert, *Miami Indians of Indiana*, 1–3.
132. Ibid., 3–4.
133. Dillon, *History of Indiana*, 14.
134. Cayton noted that the Wea, Piankashaw and Miami bands "were independent tribes, but shared the same basic cultural and social characteristics." *Frontier Indiana*, 6.

135. Rafert, *Miami Indians of Indiana*, 7.
136. Edmunds, *Shawnee Prophet*, 7.
137. Ibid.
138. Ibid.
139. Ibid., 8.
140. Wallace, "Iroquois," 15–28.
141. Ibid., 18.
142. Ibid., 22.
143. Ibid.
144. Ibid., 23.
145. Esarey, *History of Indiana*, 28.
146. Ibid.
147. Ibid., 31.
148. Cayton, *Frontier Indiana*, 27.
149. Ibid., 28.
150. Ibid., 31.
151. Rafert, *Miami Indians of Indiana*, 44.
152. Ibid.
153. Esarey, *History of Indiana*, 48.
154. Rafert, *Miami Indians of Indiana*, 44.
155. Cayton, *Frontier Indiana*, 96.
156. Esarey, *History of Indiana*, 92–125.
157. Ibid.
158. Ibid., 111–12.
159. Ibid., 92–125.
160. Cayton, *Frontier Indiana*, 166.

Chapter 5

161. Ferguson, "White River Delaware Indians," 1.
162. The Algonquian language family consists of numerous Native American languages spoken by the peoples throughout the Eastern Woodlands in the Late Pre-Contact period and Contact period. The other major language family in this area are Iroquois.
163. Ferguson, "White River Delaware Indians," 1.
164. Ibid.
165. Weslager, *Delaware Indians*, 33.
166. Ferguson, "White River Delaware Indians," 3.
167. Ibid., 4–7; Weslager, *Delaware Indians*, 45.
168. Weslager, *Delaware Indians*, 33.
169. Ferguson, "White River Delaware Indians," 2.

170. Trowbridge, *Traditions of the Lenéé Lenáúpee*, 4.
171. Ibid.
172. Schutt, *Peoples of the River Valleys*, 3.
173. Weslager, *Delaware Indians*, 37.
174. Ferguson, "White River Delaware Indians," 3.
175. Weslager, *Delaware Indians*, 33.
176. Ferguson, "White River Delaware Indians," 4.
177. Ibid.
178. Ibid.
179. Ibid., 5.
180. Ibid.
181. Ibid. Ferguson identifies Daniel Brinton and Anthony Wallace as the original researchers who postulated a Nanticoke/Unalachtigo connection.
182. Weslager, *Delaware Indians*, 47.
183. Ibid., 45.
184. Ferguson, "White River Delaware Indians," 6.
185. Ibid., 7.
186. Ibid., 8. Ferguson was identifying research completed in Harrington's 1961 *Sketch of Lenape Culture.*
187. Schutt, *Peoples of the River Valleys*, 156.
188. Ibid., 157.
189. Hodge, *Handbook of the American Indians*, 386.
190. Weslager, *Delaware Indians*, 50–76.
191. Ibid., 55.
192. Hodge, *Handbook of the American Indians*, 385.
193. Weslager, *Delaware Indians*, 62.
194. Ibid., 62–63.
195. Ibid., 42.
196. Obermeyer, *Delaware Tribe in a Cherokee Nation*, 42.
197. Trowbridge, *Traditions of the Lenéé Lenáúpee*, 6.
198. Ibid.
199. Weslager, *Delaware Indians*, 288.
200. Trowbridge, *Traditions of the Lenéé Lenáúpee*, 7.
201. Ibid.
202. Ibid.

CHAPTER 6

203. Kraft, *Delaware Indian Symposium*, 59–60.
204. Schutt, *Peoples of the River Valleys*, 51–59.
205. Ibid., 40.

206. Ibid., 41.
207. Ibid.
208. Weslager, *Delaware Indians*, 133.
209. Ibid., 113–35.
210. Schutt, *Peoples of the River Valleys*, 51–59.
211. Weslager, *Delaware Indians*, 133.
212. Ibid., 134.
213. Ibid., 180.
214. Schutt, *Peoples of the River Valleys*, 59.
215. Ibid., 62.
216. Ibid., 32.
217. Ibid.
218. Ibid., 33.
219. Weslager, *Delaware Indians*, 151.
220. Ibid., 163.
221. Ibid., 165.
222. Ibid.
223. Ibid., 170.
224. Ibid., 179.
225. Delaware Tribe of Indians, "Walking Purchase."
226. Ibid.
227. Ibid.
228. Ibid.
229. Ibid.
230. Gilbert, "What Ye Indians Call 'Ye Hurry Walk.'"
231. Schutt, *Peoples of the River Valleys*, 112.
232. Weslager, *Delaware Indians*, 224.
233. Ibid., 226.
234. Schutt, *Peoples of the River Valleys*, 117.
235. Ibid., 117–18.
236. Weslager, *Delaware Indians*, 289.
237. Schutt, *Peoples of the River Valleys*, 153.
238. Hunter, "Delaware Nativist Revival," 40.
239. Schutt, *Peoples of the River Valleys*, 117.
240. Quote taken from an e-mail exchange with philologist Ray Whritenour in November 2015.
241. Hunter, "Delaware Nativist Revival," 42.
242. Ibid., 44.
243. Ibid.
244. Weslager, *Delaware Indians*, 242.
245. Ibid., 243.
246. Schutt, *Peoples of the River Valleys*, 163.

247. Ibid.
248. Ibid., 161–62.
249. Article 6, available online at http://avalon.law.yale.edu/18th_century/del1778.asp.
250. Weslager, *Delaware Indians*, 298.
251. Ibid.
252. Ibid.
253. Ibid., 306.
254. Ibid., 308.
255. Ibid., 314.
256. Ibid.
257. Ibid., 315.
258. Ibid., 316.
259. Ibid.
260. Ibid.
261. Schutt, *Peoples of the River Valleys*, 173.
262. Ibid., 172.
263. Weslager, *Delaware Indians*, 317.
264. Ibid.
265. Sugden, *Tecumseh*, 42.
266. Jortner, *Gods of Prophetstown*, 51.
267. Trowbridge, *Traditions of the Lenéé Lenáúpee*, 3.
268. Ibid.
269. Schutt, *Peoples of the River Valleys*, 182.

CHAPTER 7

270. Weslager, *Delaware Indians*, 331.
271. Ibid., 332.
272. Ibid.
273. Dillon, *History of Indiana*, 164.
274. Ibid., 165.
275. Weslager, *Delaware Indians*, 333.
276. McCafferty, *Native American Place Names*, 88–93.
277. Ibid.
278. Ibid.
279. Thompson, *Sons of the Wilderness*, 197–207.
280. Sugden, *Tecumseh*, 99.
281. Ibid., 100.
282. Trowbridge, *Traditions of the Lenéé Lenáúpee.*

283. All information taken from Thompson, *Sons of the Wilderness*, 197–207, and from McCord and Cochran, "Ghosts of the Delaware."
284. Olson, "Kilgore 'Pact' Legend"; Olson, "'York' Indians in Indiana After 1817."
285. Weslager, *Delaware Indians*, 352.
286. Trowbridge, *Traditions of the Lenéé Lenáúpee.*
287. Sugden, *Tecumseh*, 110.
288. Stocker, *History of the Moravian Mission*, 15.
289. Ibid., 16.
290. Hart, *American History Told by Contemporaries*, 470.
291. Ibid.
292. Stocker, *History of the Moravian Mission*, 15.
293. Ibid.
294. Ibid.
295. Thompson, *Sons of the Wilderness*, 45.
296. Stocker, *History of the Moravian Mission*, 15.
297. Gipson, *Moravian Indian Mission on White River*, 23.
298. Weslager, *Delaware Indians*, 335–36; Cranor, "Kik Tha We Nun," 3.
299. Weslager, *Delaware Indians*, 335.
300. Ibid.
301. Cranor, "Kik Tha We Nun," 3. Cranor is paraphrasing the description from John Johnston.
302. Ibid., 1–14.
303. Weslager, *Delaware Indians*, 337.
304. Ibid., 337–38.
305. Ibid., 338.
306. Dillon, *History of Indiana*, 418.
307. Ibid., 430.
308. Thompson, *Sons of the Wilderness*, 50.
309. Miller, "1806 Purge Among the Indiana Delaware," 259.

CHAPTER 8

310. Gipson, *Moravian Indian Mission on White River.*
311. Esarey, *History of Indiana*, 190.
312. Dillon, *History of Indiana*, 482.
313. Unless otherwise noted, all information in this section is taken from Thompson, *Sons of the Wilderness.* Quotes are identified with page numbers in following notes.
314. Ibid., 38.
315. Ibid., 44.

316. Ibid.
317. Ibid.
318. Ibid., 80.
319. Gipson, *Moravian Indian Mission on White River*, 13.
320. Ibid.
321. Miller, "1806 Purge Among the Indiana Delaware," 257.
322. Gipson, *Moravian Indian Mission on White River*, 141.
323. Ibid., 256.
324. Thompson, *Sons of the Wilderness*, 45.
325. Gipson, *Moravian Indian Mission on White River*, 247.
326. Ibid., 314.
327. Stocker, *History of the Moravian Mission*, 69.

Chapter 9

328. Wallace, "New Religions Among the Delaware Indians."
329. Ibid.
330. Hunter, "Delaware Nativist Revival," 40.
331. Ibid., 42.
332. Ibid., 40–47.
333. Ibid., 46.
334. Ibid.
335. Miller, "Old Religion Among the Delawares," 125.
336. Ibid.
337. Hunter, "Delaware Nativist Revival," 47.
338. Gipson, *Moravian Indian Mission on White River*, 358.
339. Ibid.
340. Ibid.
341. Ibid.
342. Ibid.
343. Miller, "1806 Purge Among the Indiana Delaware," 252.
344. Gipson, *Moravian Indian Mission on White River*, 333.
345. Miller, "1806 Purge Among the Indiana Delaware," 252–53.
346. Gipson, *Moravian Indian Mission on White River*, 354
347. Miller, "1806 Purge Among the Indiana Delaware," 253.
348. Edmunds, *Shawnee Prophet*, 28.
349. Ibid.
350. Ibid., 33.
351. Ibid.
352. Ibid.
353. Ibid., 34.

354. Sugden, *Tecumseh*, 120.
355. Ibid., 121.
356. Ibid.
357. Ibid.
358. Miller, "1806 Purge Among the Indiana Delaware," 254.
359. Ibid.
360. Ibid.
361. Ibid.
362. Ibid., 256.
363. Gipson, *Moravian Indian Mission on White River*, 417.
364. Miller, "1806 Purge Among the Indiana Delaware."
365. Indiana Historical Collections, *Messages and Letters of William Henry Harrison*, vol. 1, 184.
366. Gipson, *Moravian Indian Mission on White River*, 418.
367. Sugden, *Tecumseh*, 125.
368. Miller, "1806 Purge Among the Indiana Delaware."
369. Ibid.
370. Cottman, "Indian Torture Post in Delaware County."

CHAPTER 10

371. Miller, "Old Religion Among the Delawares," 113.
372. Ibid., 114.
373. Ibid.
374. Ibid.
375. McCracken, "Delaware Big House," 185.
376. Ibid.
377. Ibid., 186.
378. Speck, *Study of the Delaware Indian Big House Ceremony*, vol. 2.
379. Miller, "Old Religion Among the Delawares," 125.
380. Ibid.
381. Miller, "1806 Purge Among the Indiana Delaware," 262.
382. McCracken, "Delaware Big House," 186.
383. Speck, *Study of the Delaware Indian Big House Ceremony*, vol. 2, 81.
384. Miller, "1806 Purge Among the Indiana Delaware," 261.
385. Feldman, *When the Mississippi Ran Backwards*.
386. Miller, "1806 Purge Among the Indiana Delaware," 261.
387. Speck, *Study of the Delaware Indian Big House Ceremony*, vol. 2, 81.

Chapter 11

388. Barce, "Governor Harrison and the Treaty of Fort Wayne," 352–67.
389. Ibid.
390. Ibid.
391. Weslager, *Delaware Indians*, 345.
392. Ibid., 347.
393. Dillon, *History of Indiana*, 463.
394. Ibid.
395. Sugden, *Tecumseh*, 229.
396. Edmunds, *Shawnee Prophet*, 119.
397. Sugden, *Tecumseh*, 237–54.
398. Dillon, *History of Indiana*, 482.
399. Ibid., 485.
400. Ibid., 486.
401. Ibid., 492.
402. Cayton, *Frontier Indiana*, 224.
403. Dillon, *History of Indiana*, 492.
404. Thompson, *Sons of the Wilderness*, 72.
405. Dillon, *History of Indiana*, 509.
406. Ibid.
407. Thompson, *Sons of the Wilderness*, 73.
408. Dillon, *History of Indiana*, 511.
409. Ibid., 514.
410. Ibid., 515.
411. Ibid., 524.
412. Ibid., 525.
413. Thompson, *Sons of the Wilderness*, 75.
414. See article 2 of the treaty.

Chapter 12

415. Weslager, *Delaware Indians*, 350.
416. Ibid., 351.
417. Olson, "Anatomy of the 1818 Treaties," 1.
418. Ibid.
419. Ibid., 10.
420. Ibid., 68.
421. Ibid.
422. Ibid., 58.
423. See article 7 of the treaty.
424. Olson, "Anatomy of the 1818 Treaties," 45.

425. McCoy, *History of Baptist Indian Missions*, 52.
426. Ibid., 55.
427. Ibid., 59.
428. Ibid.
429. Ibid., 70.
430. Introduction from James Rementer in Trowbridge, *Delaware Indian Language of 1824*, 1.
431. Ibid., 11.
432. Ibid.
433. Thompson, *Sons of the Wilderness*, 123.
434. Ibid., 121.
435. Weslager, *Delaware Indians*, 352.
436. Thompson, *Sons of the Wilderness*, 123.
437. Ibid., 123–24.
438. Weslager, *Delaware Indians*, 361.
439. Ibid.
440. Ibid., 362.
441. Ibid., 366–69.
442. Ibid.
443. Ibid., 372–74.
444. Haimbaugh, *History of Delaware County*, 245–46.
445. Ibid., 247.
446. Doerr, "Massacre at Deer Lick Creek."
447. Kemper, *Twentieth Century History of Delaware County, Indiana*, 104.
448. Stoeckel and Johnson, *Delaware County, Indiana*, 13.
449. Ibid.
450. Olson, "Anatomy of the 1818 Treaties," 43.
451. Ibid.
452. Ibid.
453. Lahrman and Johnson, "Delaware Indian's Reservation," 123.
454. Ibid.

Bibliography

Abrams, Elliot M. "Hopewell Archaeology: A View from the Northern Woodlands." *Journal of Archaeological Research* 17, no. 2 (2009): 169–204.

Archaeology Wordsmith. "Archaeology Wordsmith." http://www.archaeologywordsmith.com/index.php.

Barce, Ellmore. "Governor Harrison and the Treaty of Fort Wayne, 1809." *Indiana Magazine of History* (1915): 352–67.

Caldwell, Joseph R. *Trend and Tradition in the Prehistory of the Eastern United States.* Arlington, TX: American Anthropological Association, 1958.

Cayton, Andrew R.L. *Frontier Indiana.* Bloomington: Indiana University Press, 1998.

Clay, R. Berle. "The Essential Features of Adena Ritual and Their Implications." *Southeastern Archaeology* (1998): 1–21.

Cochran, Donald. "Culture History of Indiana." Ball State University, Muncie, IN, 2004. https://cms.bsu.edu/-/media/WWW/DepartmentalContent/AAL/ARMS20Culture20History.pdf.

Cochran, Donald R., and Beth K. McCord. "The Archaeology of Anderson Mounds, Mounds State Park, Anderson Indiana." *Reports of Investigation* 61, Archaeological Resources Management Service, Ball State University, Muncie, IN, 2001.

Connolly, Robert Patrick, and Bradley Thomas Lepper, eds. *The Fort Ancient Earthworks: Prehistoric Lifeways of the Hopewell Culture in Southwestern Ohio.* Columbus: Ohio Historical Society, 2004.

Cottman, George S. "Indian Torture Post in Delaware County." *Indiana Magazine of History* (1905).

Cranor, Ruby. "'Kik Tha We Nun': The Delaware Chief William Anderson and His Descendants." Bartlesville, Oklahoma, 1991.

Dancey, William S. *Ohio Hopewell Community Organization*. Kent, OH: Kent State University Press, 1997.

Delaware Tribe of Indians. "The Walking Purchase." http://delawaretribe.org/blog/2013/06/27/the-walking-purchase.

Diamond, Jared M., and Doug Ordunio. *Guns, Germs and Steel*. Documentary, National Geographic Society, 2005.

Dillon, John Brown. *The History of Indiana*. N.p.: W. Sheets & Company, 1843.

Doerr, Brian M. "The Massacre at Deer Lick Creek, Madison County, Indiana, 1824." *Indiana Magazine of History* (1997): 19–47.

Edmunds, R. David. *The Shawnee Prophet*. Lincoln: University of Nebraska Press, 1985.

Ehlers, Jürgen, and Philip Leonard Gibbard. *Quaternary Glaciations—Extent and Chronology—Part I: Europe*. Vol. 2. Philadelphia, PA: Elsevier, 2004.

Emerson, T.E., D.L. McElrath and A.C. Fortier, eds. *Late Woodland Societies: Tradition and Transformation Across the Midcontinent*. Lincoln: University of Nebraska Press, 2000.

Emerson, Thomas E., and R. Barry Lewis. *Cahokia and the Hinterlands: Middle Mississippian Cultures of the Midwest*. Champaign: University of Illinois Press, 1999.

Esarey, Logan. *A History of Indiana: From Its Exploration to 1850*. Vol. 1. N.p.: WK Stewart Company, 1915.

Fagan, Brian M. *The First North Americans: An Archaeological Journey*. London: Thames & Hudson, 2011.

———. *The Oxford Companion to Archaeology*. Oxford, UK: Oxford University Press, 1996.

Fagundes, Nelson J.R., Ricardo Kanitz, Roberta Eckert, Ana C.S. Valls et al. "Mitochondrial Population Genomics Supports a Single Pre-Clovis Origin with a Coastal Route for the Peopling of the Americas." *American Journal of Human Genetics* 82, no. 3 (2008): 583–92.

Feldman, Jay. *When the Mississippi Ran Backwards: Empire, Intrigue, Murder, and the New Madrid Earthquakes*. New York: Simon and Schuster, 2007.

Ferguson, Roger J. "The White River Delaware Indians: An Ethnohistoric Synthesis, 1795–1867." Thesis, Department of Education, Ball State University, 1972.

Galloway, Patricia Kay, ed. *The Hernando de Soto Expedition: History, Historiography, and "Discovery" in the Southeast*. Lincoln: University of Nebraska Press, 2006.

Gilbert, Daniel. "What Ye Indians Call 'Ye Hurry Walk.'" Pennsylvania Center for the Book, Penn State University, fall of 2009. http://pabook.libraries.psu.edu/palitmap/WalkingPurchase.html.

Gipson, L.H. *The Moravian Indian Mission on White River: Diaries and Letters, May 5, 1799, to November 12, 1806*. Indiana Historical Collections, 1938.

Graham, Colin D., and Robert McCullough. "Archaeological Investigation of Two Western Basin Tradition-Related Sites in Northeast and Central Indiana—Vol. I: Kramer Enclosure (12-Al-15); Vol. II: Castor Farm (12-H-3). Reports of Investigations 1001." Indiana University—Purdue University, Fort Wayne, 2010.

Haimbaugh, Frank D. *History of Delaware County, Indiana in Two Volumes.* Indianapolis, IN: Historical Publishing Company, n.d.

Hart, Albert Bushnell. *American History Told by Contemporaries: Era of Colonization, 1492–1689.* N.p.: Minerva Group Inc., 2002.

Hays, Christopher T. "Adena Mortuary Patterns in Central Ohio." *Southeastern Archaeology* 29, no. 1 (2010): 106–20.

Herrmann, Edward W., G. William Monaghan, William F. Romain, Timothy M. Schilling et al. "A New Multistage Construction Chronology for the Great Serpent Mound, USA." *Journal of Archaeological Science* 50 (2014): 117–25.

Hodge, Frederick Webb, ed. *Handbook of American Indians North of Mexico, NZ.* Vol. 30. Washington, D.C.: U.S. Government Printing Office, 1912.

Howe, Henry. *Historical Collections of Ohio, in Two Volumes: An Encyclopedia of the State.* Vol. 1. N.p.: State of Ohio, 1907.

Huckell, Bruce B., and J. David Kilby, eds. *Clovis Caches: Recent Discoveries and New Research.* Albuquerque: University of New Mexico Press, 2014.

Hunter, Charles E. "The Delaware Nativist Revival of the Mid-Eighteenth Century." *Ethnohistory* (1971): 39–49.

Indiana Department of Education. *Indiana Academic Standards and Resource Guide Grade 4 Indiana in the Nation and the World.* 2013. http://www.doe.in.gov/sites/default/files/standards/socialstudies/ss-2014-res-gr4-20150317.pdf.

Indiana Department of Natural Resources Division of Historic Preservation and Archaeology. *Indiana Archaeology* 6, no. 1 (n.d.): 67. http://www.in.gov/dnr/historic/files/hp-Vol6_No1_Indiana_Archaeology.pdf.

Indiana Historical Collections. *Messages and Letters of William Henry Harrison.* Vol. 1. N.p.: Indiana Historical Commission, 1922.

Jortner, Adam. *The Gods of Prophetstown: The Battle of Tippecanoe and the Holy War for the American Frontier.* Oxford, UK: Oxford University Press, 2011.

Kaufman, D.S., and W.F. Manley. "Quaternary Glaciations—Extent and Chronology, Part II: North America." *Developments in Quaternary Science* 2 (2004): 9–27.

Kellar, James H. *An Introduction to the Prehistory of Indiana.* Indianapolis: Indiana Historical Society, 1983.

Kemper, General William Harrison. *A Twentieth Century History of Delaware County, Indiana.* Vol. 2. N.p.: Lewis Publishing Company, 1908.

Kilby, J. David. *An Investigation of Clovis Caches: Content, Function, and Technological Organization.* Albuquerque: University of New Mexico, 2008.

Kluge, John Peter, and Abraham Luckenbach. *The Moravian Indian Mission on White River: Diaries and Letters, May 5, 1799, to November 12, 1806*. Edited by Lawrence Henry Gipson. N.p.: Indiana Historical Bureau, 1938.

Knight, Vernon J., Lawrence A. Clayton and Edward Carter Moore, eds. *The De Soto Chronicles: The Expedition of Hernando de Soto to North America in 1539–1543*. Tuscaloosa: University of Alabama Press, 1993.

Kraft, Herbert C., ed. *A Delaware Indian Symposium*. No. 4. Pennsylvania Historical Society, 1974.

Lahrman, Dolores M., and Ross S. Johnson. "A Delaware Indian's Reservation: Samuel Cassman vs. Goldsmith C. Gilbert." *Indiana Magazine of History* (1975): 103–23.

Madison, James H. *Hoosiers: A New History of Indiana*. Bloomington: Indiana University Press, 2014.

Mann, Charles C. *1491: New Revelations of the Americas before Columbus*. New York: Alfred A. Knopf, 2005.

———. *1493: Uncovering the New World Columbus Created*. New York: Alfred A. Knopf, 2011.

McCafferty, Michael. *Native American Place Names of Indiana*. Champaign: University of Illinois Press, 2008.

McCord, Beth. "1999 Excavations at Mounds State Park (12-M-2) and the New Castle Site (12-Hn-1)." Reports of Investigation 73, Archaeological Resources Management Service, Ball State University, Muncie, IN, 2001.

McCord, Beth K., and D. Cochran. *The Fudge Site: A New Look at an Ancient Monument, Randolph County, Indiana*. Archaeological Resources Management Service, Ball State University, Muncie, IN, 2006.

———. "The Ghosts of the Delaware: An Archaeological Study of Delaware Settlement Along the White River, Indiana." *Reports of Investigation* 62. Archaeological Resource Management Service, Ball State University, Muncie, IN, 2002.

———. "The New Castle Site Revisited." Archaeological Resources Management Service, Ball State University, Muncie, IN, 1999.

———. "Woodland Sites in East Central Indiana: A Survey and Evaluation." Archaeological Resources Management Services, Ball State University, Muncie, IN, 1996.

McCord, Beth K., and Donald R. Cochran. "The Adena Complex: Identity and Context in East-Central Indiana." *Transitions: Archaic and Early Woodland Research in the Ohio Country* (2008): 334–60.

———. "An Archaeological Survey of the Taylor Property at the Strawtown Prairie, Hamilton County, Indiana." Archaeological Resources Management Service, Ball State University, Muncie, IN, 2003.

McCoy, Isaac. *History of Baptist Indian Missions*. N.p.: Morrison, 1840.

McCracken, Horace L. "The Delaware Big House." *Chronicles of Oklahoma* 34 (1956): 183–92.

McCullough, Robert. "Cultural Interaction Along the West Fork of the White River During the Late Prehistoric Period." In *Facing the Final Millennium: Studies in the Late Prehistory of Indiana, A.D. 700 to 1700*. Indianapolis: Indiana Department of Natural Resources, Division of Historic Preservation and Archaeology, 2003.

Miller, Jay. "The 1806 Purge Among the Indiana Delaware: Sorcery, Gender, Boundaries, and Legitimacy." *Ethnohistory* (1994): 245–66.

———. "Old Religion Among the Delawares: The Gamwing (Big House Rite)." *Ethnohistory* (1997): 113–34.

Milner, George R. *The Moundbuilders: Ancient Peoples of Eastern North America*. Vol. 110. London: Thames & Hudson, 2004.

Mithen, Steven. *After the Ice: A Global Human History, 20,000–5000 BC*. London: Weidenfeld & Nicolson, 2011.

Nolan, Kevin C., and Steven P. Howard. "Using Evolutionary Archaeology and Evolutionary Ecology to Explain Cultural Elaboration: The Case of Middle Ohio Valley Woodland Period Ceremonial Subsistence." *North American Archaeologist* 31, no. 2 (2010): 119–54.

Obermeyer, Brice. *Delaware Tribe in a Cherokee Nation*. Lincoln: University of Nebraska Press, 2009.

———. "Removal and the Cherokee-Delaware Agreement." In *Delaware Tribe in a Cherokee Nation*. Lincoln: University of Nebraska Press, 2009.

Olson, Andrew Arthur. "Anatomy of the 1818 Treaties of St. Mary's and the 'New Purchase' of Indiana." Unpublished, 2011.

———. "The Kilgore 'Pact' Legend." Unpublished, 2011.

———. "'York' Indians in Indiana After 1817: Brotherton, Stockbridge & Musee—Delaware." Unpublished, 2010.

Otto, M.P., and B.G. Redmond. *Transitions: Archaic and Early Woodland Research in the Ohio Country*. Athens: Ohio University Press, 2008.

Pauketat, Timothy R. *Cahokia: Ancient America's Great City on the Mississippi*. New York: Penguin, 2009.

Peckham, H.H. *Indiana: A History*. Champaign: University of Illinois Press, 1978.

Rafert, Stewart. *The Miami Indians of Indiana: A Persistent People, 1654–1994*. Indianapolis: Indiana Historical Society, 1996.

Romain, William F. *Shamans of the Lost World: A Cognitive Approach to the Prehistoric Religion of the Ohio Hopewell*. Lanham, MD: Rowman & Littlefield, 2009.

Schutt, Amy C. *Peoples of the River Valleys: The Odyssey of the Delaware Indians*. Philadelphia: University of Pennsylvania Press, 2013.

Silverberg, Robert. *The Mound Builders*. Athens: Ohio University Press, 1986.

Smith, Bruce D., and Richard A. Yarnell. "Initial Formation of an Indigenous Crop Complex in Eastern North America at 3800 BP." *Proceedings of the National Academy of Sciences* 106, no. 16 (2009): 6,561–66.

Speck, Frank G. *A Study of the Delaware Indian Big House Ceremony: In Native Text Dictated by Witapanóxwe*. Vol. 2. N.p.: Pennsylvania Historical Commission, 1931.

Stanford, D.J., and B.A. Bradley. *Across Atlantic Ice: The Origin of America's Clovis Culture*. Berkeley: University of California Press, 2012.

Stocker, Harry Emilius. *History of the Moravian Mission Among the Indians on the White River in Indiana*. N.p.: Times Publishing Company, 1917.

Stoeckel, Althea Lucille, and Ross S. Johnson, eds. *Delaware County, Indiana, 1827–1850: The Pioneer Period*. Muncie, IN: Ball State University, 1975.

Sugden, John. *Tecumseh: A Life*. London: Macmillan Publishers, 1999.

Tankersley, Kenneth B., Edward E. Smith and Donald R. Cochran. "Early Paleoindian Land Use, Mobility, and Lithic Exploitation Patterns: An Updated Distribution of Fluted Points in Indiana." *North American Archaeologist* 11, no. 4 (1991): 301–19.

Thompson, Charles Nebeker. *Sons of the Wilderness, John and William Conner*. Vol. 12. Indianapolis: Indiana Historical Society, 1987.

Trowbridge, Charles. *Delaware Indian Language of 1824*. American Language Reprints Supplement. Introduction from James Rementer. N.p.: Evolution Publishing and Manufacturing, 2011.

———. *Traditions of the Lenéé Lenáûpee or Delawares*, 1823. Typed from the original document by James Rementer. Available at the Bentley Historical Library, University of Michigan in "C.C. Trowbridge Papers."

Vickery, Kent D. "'Reluctant' or 'Avant-Garde' Hopewell?: Suggestions of Middle Woodland Culture Change in East-Central Indiana and South-Central Ohio." In "In Hopewell Archaeology: The Chillicothe Conference." Edited by D.S. Brose and N'omi Greber. *Midcontinental Journal of Archaeology—Special Papers* 3 (1979): 86–93.

Wallace, Anthony F.C. "New Religions Among the Delaware Indians, 1600–1900." *Southwestern Journal of Anthropology* (1956): 1–21.

Wallace, Paul A.W. "The Iroquois: A Brief Outline of Their History." *Pennsylvania History* (1956): 15–28.

Weslager, C.A. *The Delaware Indians: A History*. New Brunswick: Rutgers University Press, 1989.

Willey, Gordon R., and Philip Phillips. *Method and Theory in American Archaeology*. Tuscaloosa: University Alabama Press, 1958.

Witthoft, John, and William A. Hunter. "The Seventeenth-Century Origins of the Shawnee." *Ethnohistory* 2, no. 1 (1955): 42–57.

Woodward, Susan L., and Jerry N. McDonald. *Indian Mounds of the Middle Ohio Valley: A Guide to Adena and Ohio Hopewell Sites*. Granville, OH: McDonald and Woodward Publishing Company, 1986.

Index

A

B

C

D

F

Y

Z

About the Author

Chris Flook is a lecturer of telecommunications at Ball State University. He teaches documentary filmmaking, web design and motion graphics. In recent years, he has advised student teams in the production of several documentaries, including *The Lenape on the Wapahani*, *A Legacy Etched in Glass* and *Indiana Crossrails: A Transit Choice*. Flook is also the vice-president of the Delaware County Historical Society and is on the board for the Indiana Barn Foundation.

Visit us at
www.historypress.net

This title is also available as an e-book